A Percentage of the Take

Other books by Walter Goodman

THE CLOWNS OF COMMERCE

ALL HONORABLE MEN

THE COMMITTEE

BLACK BONDAGE

A
PERCENTAGE
OF THE
TAKE

Walter Goodman

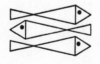

Farrar, Straus and Giroux

NEW YORK

For Elaine, after twenty years

Contents

Characters

(ARRANGED IN ORDER OF THEIR APPEARANCE, MORE OR LESS)

JAMES L. MARCUS, *New York City's Commissioner of Water Supply, Gas and Electricity. Friend of Mayor John V. Lindsay*

HERBERT ITKIN, *a lawyer. Friend of James Marcus*

CHARLES J. RAPPAPORT, *a lawyer. Protégé of Herbert Itkin*

The Mortgage Loan

JAMES (JIMMY DOYLE) PLUMERI, *a racketeer. Associate of Herbert Itkin*

SAMUEL BERGER, *a one-time union official*

FRANK ZULFERINO, *a union president*

SHIAH ARSHAM, *a needy businessman*

Conestoga Investments, Ltd.

ALBERT M. GREENFIELD, JR., *a well-to-do Philadelphia real-estate man, active in Democratic politics*

PETER W. LITTMAN, *brother-in-law of Albert Greenfield*

The Jerome Park Reservoir Bribe

DANIEL J. MOTTO, *a union president. Associate of Herbert Itkin*

CARL D'ANGELO, *a lawyer. Friend of Daniel Motto*

ARMAND D'ANGELO, *former New York City Commissioner of Water Supply, Gas and Electricity. Father of Carl*

HENRY FRIED, *millionaire contractor—head of S. T. Grand; Triboro Carting; Mackay Construction; Mackay Trucking*

ANTONIO (TONY DUCKS) CORALLO, *a racketeer. Associate of Daniel Motto*

JOSEPH P. PIZZO, *deceased, a "labor-relations consultant." Friend of Antonio Corallo and associate of Henry Fried*

Tangential Operations

VINCENT F. ALBANO, JR., *Chairman, New York Republican County Committee. Close associate of Mayor Lindsay and intermediary for Henry Fried*

JOSEPH RUGGIERO, *a New York Republican Party politician. Intermediary for Oakhill Contracting*

ERNEST MUCCINI & son—*owners of Oakhill Contracting*

EDWARD A. ORLANDO & father—*owners of N. A. Orlando Contracting*

VINCENT GRILLO; WILLIAM MOULTRAY; GUS (BUDDY) SPATAFORA—*partners in Vintray-Orlando-Daril*

MICHAEL BONFONDEO, *a loan shark*

The Consolidated Edison Conspiracy

MILTON LIPKINS, *a businessman—Broadway Maintenance Company*

MAX M. ULRICH, *a vice-president of Consolidated Edison. Acquaintance of Milton Lipkins*

GERALD R. HADDEN, *a vice-president of Consolidated Edison. Privately associated with Henry Fried*

SYDNEY BARON, *a "public-relations consultant" for Consolidated Edison. Associate of Max Ulrich. Confidant of Carmine De Sapio*

CARMINE G. DE SAPIO, *a once-powerful Democratic politician. Friend of Henry Fried*

CHARLES E. EBLE, *former president of Consolidated Edison*

CHARLES F. LUCE, *president of Consolidated Edison*

Elizabeth Street police station, June 26, 1968. The booking of Herbert Itkin and James L. Marcus

UPI

WIDE WORLD

F.B.I. headquarters, December 18, 1968. Under arrest: Antonio (Tony Ducks) Corallo (LEFT) and Henry Fried (RIGHT)

(OPPOSITE PAGE, TOP) *City Hall, March 11, 1966. The swearing in of James Marcus as assistant to the Mayor*

(OPPOSITE PAGE, BOTTOM) *St. Clement's Episcopal Church, January 15, 1967. The christening of George Griswold Frelinghuysen Marcus —held by his godfather, John Vliet Lindsay*

(ABOVE) *F.B.I. headquarters, December 18, 1967. Daniel J. Motto* (LEFT) *and Charles J. Rappaport* (RIGHT)

(BELOW) *Hotel Astor, September 16, 1963. Vincent F. Albano, Jr.,* (CENTER) *is congratulated by New York State Attorney General Louis Lefkowitz and Senator Jacob K. Javits on his election as Chairman of the New York Republican Committee*

Jerome Park reservoir, May 11, 1967. Mayor Lindsay and Commissioner Marcus arrive for the refilling

(ABOVE) *Loyalty Parade, April 29, 1961. Carmine G. De Sapio* (LEFT) *and Mayor Robert F. Wagner with the Queen of the Day*

(BELOW) *Federal Courthouse, December 13, 1969. The jury has returned its verdict*

(ABOVE) *Consolidated Edison offices, March 28, 1967. Charles F. Luce* (LEFT) *talks about his appointment as head of the company. Listening* (RIGHT) *is outgoing chairman Charles E. Eble. The middleman is Max M. Ulrich*

(BELOW) *Federal Courthouse, November 28, 1969. Gerald R. Hadden* (LEFT) *arrives, with lawyer, to testify against Carmine De Sapio, et al.*

NEW YORK TIMES

Lewisburg, Pa., Federal Prison, September 13, 1968

"The politician who steals is worse than a thief. He is a fool. With the grand opportunities all around for the man with a political pull, there's no excuse for stealin' a cent."

PLUNKITT OF TAMMANY HALL

A Percentage of the Take

Introduction

SEVENTY years ago, the Order of Acorns, a body of New York reformers who counted Mark Twain among their number, observed: "New Yorkers' eyes have grown so dim, they see nothing duller than a lightning stroke." It is not often that we are privileged to make use of so bright a stroke as the Marcus affair. In illuminating the activities not only of a high public official but of a millionaire businessman, an officer of a labor union, a delegate from the Mafia, a major executive of a major company, a big-time politician, a special breed of confidence man, and assorted contractors, politicos, lawyers, and go-betweens, it opens to our inspection the way certain kinds of things get done in a big city and the kinds of men who do them.

The outlines of our story are clear. In 1965 James Marcus, young man on the make, joins the new Lindsay administration as Commissioner of Water Supply, Gas and Electricity. His position is high enough to allow play to all his weaknesses, and in the improbable Herbert Itkin he finds the man for his season. Falling in with Herbert Itkin was a remarkable bit of fortune for Marcus—but in the normal course of his duties he would in any case have met

Henry Fried and Carmine De Sapio and most of the others whose names appear in the following pages. They were all there, courtier-pimps watching for a wink from my lord of the water supply. The two best-advertised cases of bribes being passed to Marcus-Itkin were related to an $800,000 contract to clean the Jerome Park reservoir in the Bronx and to a complex scheme involving the giant Consolidated Edison Company, but there were others as well. At the hour it became known that they were on the take, Marcus-Itkin found that the machinery they needed was already in existence, oiled up and suitable for immediate service. And there was no shortage of customers.

The Marcus story, divulged in intriguing segments over a period of two years, has been diligently reported in the daily press. Still, there is value, I think, in trying to put the cases together in one place and in a more comprehensive and comprehensible way than newspapers can by their nature manage. It is a good story, and it may give us a fuller sense of the mechanics of corruption as practiced in New York and elsewhere. The tale of the amiably vicious alliance that feeds upon our cities does not begin and end with James Marcus and Herbert Itkin. Indeed, what makes this pair special is that they were *unsound*. Had they only known how to behave, Marcus might still be a municipal official and Henry Fried, the contractor, and Carmine De Sapio, the political mover, would be happier men. We owe our glimpse into the enduring system of favors, pressures, and bribes to an odd set of circumstances —and the reader may be left wondering how many deals are completed around the land each day in which no revealing accident intervenes.

The story is not without humor or invitations to irony,

far from it—yet in the end it can only reinforce our sourest notions of the way the city's business is conducted and the quality of the people who conduct it. No week passes without confirmation from some part of the country that thieves patrol the corridors of our public buildings and their accomplices occupy the inner offices. Where the public trust is concerned, the rich, the poor, the great middle class alike are given to betrayal—although here, as elsewhere, equality of opportunity remains a dream. The affair of Water Commissioner James Marcus, though a good catch, provides an unexotic species of fish. More like flounder than sea monster. And therein lies its significance.

In his great history, Gibbon speaks with some relief of the creatures who simply "disappeared from the knowledge of mankind." Our cast will disappear faster than most—but their like will remain, hanging around, sniffing out the main chance, grabbing what they can, and sniffing, sniffing. Nothing new in this, nothing at all. By any measure of city politicking, the late nineteen-sixties were mild and the Lindsay administration was clean. The mayor was unlucky in James Marcus, but insofar as the fault can be laid to John Lindsay for choosing his favorites without scrutinizing their references, it seems merely to have been a form of that social snobbery which exempts the son-in-law of a Lodge from the kind of questions that ordinary job applicants must suffer. It is a fault of silly manners rather than of bad character, and will more often result in official ineptitude than in official venality.

Anyone who has looked into the history of New York and the history of many other cities, and nations as well, must in fairness conclude that conditions are better than they used to be. Most officials are more honest, and the dishonest ones are more discreet; greater pains must be taken to camouflage the payoff process. But it can also be argued that in the periods of the grossest corruption—the Tweed era, the Crocker era, the heyday of Jimmy Walker —the city was still young enough to roll with the punches. New York is no longer young; it is nearly a century older than when Lord Bryce suggested that it was virtually ungovernable. Its troubles, and the troubles of cities throughout the country, have been sufficiently lamented, and there is no need to groan over them here. They might be beyond cure even if New York were run by public servants of the most superior abilities and exalted consciences, who had to do with none but highly principled private citizens. Our story suggests how far we are from that condition. The small leaks that can be tolerated when the reservoir is full become scandalous in a time of drought.

This is a New York story, but the failures and betrayals at its heart are much older than New York. It would be comforting, in a way, to believe that our national emphasis on individual success, often at the expense of personal honor, breeds corruption. In evidence of this, anticapitalist ideologists can point out that though Herbert Itkin may have been a freak and James Marcus may have been a fluke (if not a flounder), legitimate businessmen competed to meet their terms. We live, conspicuously, in a nation of men and groups that seek by whatever means to advance their particular interests . . . but who can name the socialist land where corruption has lost its meaning? The ailment is age-old and worldwide, the curse of Ancient Rome as of modern Ghana. It mocks ideology, troubling Spain no less than Russia. In our own time and place, the citizen's loyalty, like a cheap rubber band, seems too thin to stretch beyond his family and closest friends. In time of catastrophe, he is touched and his old clothes are quickly boxed and shipped off to hurricane victims. In time of emergency, when the power fails, we can find him at his neighbor's side with a flashlight. But the fit passes; each goes his own way.

"Alienation" is not the word that springs to the tongue when one speaks of Henry Fried or Daniel Motto or Carmine De Sapio. Indeed, the big businessman and the shoddy union official and the political boss are prominent in the gallery of types that the young proclaim they are alienated from. But though our racketeers and their collaborators, great boosters of the system they exploit, are not about to take to the streets in the ranks of the disaffected, their alienation goes deep. To be sure, they have warm family feelings. (One of the memorable moments in this history occurs when Daniel Motto, whose custom it was to pick up his wife each evening after her day's work, considerately leaves her sitting in their car while he walks off to pass a bribe to Herbert Itkin out of her sight.) But that seems to exhaust their sense of solidarity. It is possible that Mafia chieftains support all the orphanages in southern Italy; for native-born adults, however, the price of a loan is two percent a week.

Few of us are loan sharks—but that is not to say that our sense of community goes much deeper than that of anointed racketeers like Antonio Corallo or James Plumeri. The reader may find it difficult to leave this story convinced that what the politicians Vincent Albano and Joseph Ruggiero tried to do for Henry Fried and other contractors was in any way out of the ordinary. Had they resisted the Frieds, *that* would have been extraordinary.

At every level of political power, invidious convention rules. Nor can we solace ourselves with the belief that the numerous businessmen who sought an understanding with Marcus-Itkin were mutants; or that there was anything singular about a reform candidate going to a Daniel Motto for political support; or that the death of Joseph Pizzo has ended for once and all his interpretation of the role of "labor consultant"; or that no executive before or after Gerald Hadden, lately a vice-president of Consolidated Edison, ever accepted cash from a favor-seeking business-man; or that suspicion is unwarranted on finding a high municipal official of many years' tenure in close converse with Mafiosi; or that, as things go in the world, Carmine De Sapio carried dishonesty to an extreme. The De Sapios and the Mottos and the rest have their functions, and they find clients wherever they look.

Against the nibbling conspiracies, so destructive of all notions of a commonwealth, we have our laws. But, as Gibbon reminded us, "the operation of the wisest laws is imperfect and precarious. They seldom inspire virtue and cannot always restrain vice. Their power is insufficient to prohibit all that they condemn, nor can they always punish the actions which they prohibit." For punishment, for prohibition, for restraint, and certainly for inspiration, we must depend on men, and men have a proven tendency to be . . . if not corrupt, then amenable. One does not look for trouble. One does not wish to be put down as a *naïf*.

If James Marcus could have roused himself at some point in his unhappy career to say, "I'm sorry, but I can't take a bribe or even do you a favor, because, you see, I hold a position of public trust," Daniel Motto would have been baffled—or, more likely, he would have concluded that the commissioner had a better thing going. So would Henry Fried. And so would the greater part of the citizenry. We are cynical of our officials, not only because we know them so well but because we know ourselves and what we are capable of, given the opportunity. Lawyers, doctors, accountants, shopkeepers, truck drivers, clerks, cops—who can resist a deal? Especially at the expense of "the city"? We are deprived of whatever consolation we might have taken from the knowledge that, as things go and have gone in New York, James Marcus cannot be acclaimed a great crook, by the recognition that we are a community of small crooks. Which is to say, scarcely a community at all. It has turned out as Melville foresaw— where the wolves are killed off, the foxes increase. *Not a single contractor in New York appears to have turned away from the chance of a fix.* Where is the consolation in knowing that this, or worse, would have been the case a hundred years ago?

Cutting a corner, slipping through a loophole, making a killing, putting one over, we squeeze what we can out of each other—and, if this story is at all representative, we don't even find much pleasure in the game. Profitable it may sometimes be, but flat and stale it surely is. Our chiseling has lost its kick, like the booze in *The Iceman Cometh*. That may be a hint of imminent redemption, or it may just mean that the Iceman has arrived and settled down in City Hall.

ONE

The City Official

"I don't know the rules."
JAMES L. MARCUS

IN the middle of his life's journey, James Marcus found himself in a dark wood. He entered it after a fine bright year of success, the only completely successful year that he was to know. That came in 1965, when he was thirty-five years old and a volunteer in John Lindsay's campaign to be mayor of New York City. The Lindsay candidacy, an attack on the city's political masters, had to be run by outsiders, many of them new to municipal give and take, and James Marcus was one of these. He did the odd jobs that came his way—mainly following up potential sources of funds and support—and he won, along with the friendship of the new mayor, a place in the City Hall establishment. For the first time in his life, he could look forward to a position of consequence.

Until that good year, Marcus had played the part of the charming failure. He grew up in Schenectady, only child of a middle-class Jewish family. His father was a lawyer and sometime assistant district attorney; his mother a busy worker in a variety of causes. In his teens, owing to parental hopes for his future or exasperation with his scholastic past, he was sent off to military school, one of those places where characters are supposedly built. His later years at Union College and at the University of Pennsylvania were a blend of social success and academic failure. He found that he was better suited to the softer pleasures of the campus than to the rigors of the classroom; his record spotted with F's and cuts, he was dropped from both institutions. The jobs he held after finishing with college were of the sort that make impressive reading on a fellow's résumé but are not otherwise sustaining. He was president of a short-lived investment firm in Chicago called James, Martin & Co., which never made any money. "It was a one-man operation, overhead extremely limited, a ten-by-ten office," reports the firm's secretary-treasurer. In 1960, according to the information released when he joined the Lindsay team, he became president of Chlorodyne Chemical Company, an organization that no one has been able to track down. In 1962 he got his fanciest connection, becoming head of a subsidiary of the large and famous advertising agency, Interpublic, Inc. The subsidiary, however—called Investors Marketing Services and designed to "assist" investors—was another small operation that did not last very long. Still, it had its uses. In a press release a few years later which Marcus carried personally from City Hall to newspaper offices, this connection would be splendidly embellished by memory: Marcus described himself as having been "president of the I.M.S. subsidiary of Interpublic, Inc., a worldwide advertising and public-relations concern." Like a new wine in an old bottle, the Marcus career seemed inviting until uncorked.

Yet Marcus had charm. He cut a handsome figure, his boyish face improved by the early gray of his hair. He took pains with his grooming and his tailoring, his style up to date but not unduly innovative, appropriate, say, to a knowing young executive in a stock-brokerage house. An acquaintance of the time describes him: "He was nice and neat. Always had a suntan, always looked like he just came out of the shower." His presence was agreeable, his manner plausible, yet he seems not to have inspired great confidence: "He had a slow, almost remote way. He was this kind of guy—if you gave him a slip of paper to meet you at six o'clock, he might lose it. You couldn't be sure he'd meet you. Not the most dependable guy in the world. He tried to say yes to everybody. A nice *schlimazel*. The last guy in the world you'd figure to be capable of plotting or conniving."

Marcus was naturally attracted to affluent and swinging young New Yorkers. He gained entrance into their delectable ambiance with his marriage, in June 1962, to Lily Lodge, daughter of John Davis Lodge, former governor of Connecticut and ambassador to Spain. (Thereafter, Marcus would sometimes have himself introduced as "the son-in-law of former Connecticut Governor John Davis Lodge," or a mouthful of words to that effect. The former governor, for his part, is not known to have advertised the new connection.) Jim and Lily had met at a theatrical colony in Maine. It is understood that John Davis did not rejoice in his daughter's marriage to the upward-mobile Jew with neither personal nor professional credentials, yet the young pair seemed happy in one another. For Marcus, the social animal, this marriage opened up remarkable vistas. He was the kid before the plate-glass window, and all at once the glass was removed. Even his career seemed to take a turn for the better—not that it could easily have taken a turn for the worse: it was shortly after his marriage that he connected with Interpublic, that "worldwide advertising and public-relations concern." (An acquaintance of the period recalls him as the kind of fellow who liked to expatiate on his know-how in such matters as swinging a good deal on an apartment in New York.)

Among the new friends whom he owed to Lily was John Lindsay, then congressman from New York's Silk Stocking District. They met in 1964, and Marcus, free of worldly commitments, became a volunteer in the estimable young politician's 1965 mayoralty campaign. He was no major strategist, but his social talents served him well in making contacts in his candidate's behalf. Without the Lodge key, we may fairly assume, the doors of New York Republicanism would not have opened so wide to Marcus, so disastrously wide. "I thought he was the very nice son-in-law of a wealthy Christian family," a Lindsay aide of the time recalls dryly. Though short of the stamina that would have been required to work his way up through established party ranks, in the Lindsay camp he found a ready welcome. He owed his quick progress to the lack of an operating political machine, as well as to Lindsay's predilection for young men cast in his own handsome mold; he was in fact one of the earliest products of 1965 reform politics in New York City. Once Marcus won the friendship of John Lindsay and became a person to be reckoned with, he was doomed. He might have been spared the tribulations that lay ahead if only no one had considered him worth corrupting.

But the relationship with Lindsay developed, personally as well as professionally, and that relationship would give the events to come a dimension not usually found in New York City scandals. In January 1967 the mayor would serve as godfather at the christening of Marcus's second son, the service being held in an Episcopal church, which got little George Griswold Frelinghuysen Marcus over *that* hurdle at least. The child was further celebrated at a party in Gracie Mansion. For the first months after the election victory in November 1965, Marcus served as administration trouble shooter. He represented the city on the Delaware River Basin Commission in a dry season, and was assigned the additional task of improving the tone of Greenwich Village and the Times Square area. Marcus's sudden investment with such responsibilities suits Tocqueville's observation that in America "men undertake to direct the fortunes of the state only when they doubt their capacity to manage their private affairs."

New York's depleted water reservoirs made a lively campaign issue in the summer of 1965, and John Lindsay promised that, if elected, he would oust the water commissioner and replace him with a professional engineer. Regarding the water shortage, campaigner Lindsay declared, "Let the responsibility fall where it should—at the highest level," and he promised to "clean out the whole crew and get qualified professional engineers in the water department from the top to the bottom." At the top, Mayor Lindsay decided to install James Marcus. Why Marcus? Three or four qualified men were offered the post, but all declined. "Marcus was available," shrugs an important member of the early Lindsay team. "He was hanging around. No doubt there were better people for the job, but we were busy and they weren't on hand. Jim was."

No one checked on Marcus's educational or professional achievements before he was named Commissioner of Water Supply, Gas and Electricity, with the assured prospect of moving on to head the Environmental Protection Administration, one of ten superagencies created under the Lindsay government reorganization plan. Marcus, the perennial dropout, was in fact no less qualified in engineering than he was in any given field, but that did not matter one way or the other. Municipal commissionerships are by tradition political offices. Responsibility for the day-to-day running of the city's complex departments is vested in civil servants—engineers, accountants, and the like—who carry on their technical functions from administration to administration. Come Republican or Democrat, New Yorkers must have their water. The commissioner, however, is traditionally the mayor's man; he owes his job to a combination of past debts, prospective favors, and personal judgment that defies analysis. Recent mayors, as Theodore Lowi has noted, more and more have had to face "the alternatives of *either* a party-loyal commissioner *or* a skilled and experienced one." Lindsay, the victorious insurgent, showed a genuine interest in recruiting specialists such as Mitchell Sviridoff, Mitchell I. Ginsberg, Merril Eisenbud, Thomas P. F. Hoving, and August Heckscher. (By the beginning of his second term, he was making more appointments from among political supporters, the specialists having shown a want of staying power.) What Lindsay hoped to find in Marcus in 1966 was a mayor-loyal commissioner, with perhaps some undeveloped skills. He had assisted in the campaign; he was young and personable; he was a friend; he was, more or less, a Lodge. Turning him into a commissioner was at once politically sound and personally satisfying. If John Lindsay, the Republican in a Democratic city, could trust anyone, he could trust Jim Marcus. Only there was no one to tell Marcus, as Lorenzo de' Medici told his second son, Giovanni, as he departed for the papal court, "You are going into a sink of vice, and you will find it hard to conduct yourself decently."

Although he became an official assistant to the mayor in March 1966, charged with running the Department of Water Supply, Gas and Electricity, with its three thousand employees, Marcus would not go onto the city's payroll until he was sworn in as commissioner the following September. For the time being, therefore, he was on no one's payroll. "I never knew what he did for a living," says a co-worker. "I just assumed he had money." It was not a question of going hungry—but the situation did have its delicate aspects. The reward of marriage to a Lodge and friendship with the Lindsay (who perhaps got a feeling of security from having at his side an associate who could scorn salary) was a welcome to a very expensive stratum of New York society. The co-worker again: "He didn't socialize much with the rest of us. He was never at my house and I was never at his. I think he preferred show-business people." To live up fully to his own appreciation of his new role, Marcus needed a lot of money.

In 1966, the unsalaried Marcus did what any smart young fellow would do under the circumstances—he played the stock market. His generation has made playing the market a great national obsession. The appeals are not so different from those that make the numbers game a major urban industry, albeit for a different class—the kick of the gamble, the hope of a killing. And there is more, related to the socially sanctioned amorality of the market. Every plunger has his tips; every one is able to think of himself, at moments anyway, as an insider, operating where the action is, casting his net into the mysterious center of the unfathomable waters known as the capitalist system. There are billions down there, and no day goes by without a new tale of riches being drawn up by the acquaintance of an acquaintance. And all one needs is the tip. In the democracy of the market, the philosopher has no advantage over the dress salesman. The treasure does not ask to see a man's college degree or his intelligence quotient. One may, if one is so inclined, read the expert books on market strategy, but every plunger knows that what counts is the tip, the great equalizer, and every barber may come upon a tip, every cab driver will certainly pass one along. How much more likely then that the traveler in smart circles, the same man who may know nothing yet knows everybody, would come upon a tip that would make his fortune? A mutual-fund specialist whom Marcus visited frequently to discuss tips remembers him as "always wheeling, but incompetent at it." He adds: "If he recommended a stock, you could be sure it was nothing, a waste of a half hour."

Having discovered early that he was not cut out for workaday accomplishments, yet smitten with visions of high-riding success, Marcus was drawn insensibly to the magic of the market—that Great Reformatory for Crooks, in Finley Peter Dunne's opinion—and all that it promised. A friend recalls: "He was talking in the beginning, he was going to make five or six million dollars before two years were out." Though his investment-firm connections came to nothing, the rising stock prices of the early nineteen-sixties enabled him to do well enough with his own speculations to carry on the game at quite high stakes for a man without an income. In the spring of 1966, at the height of his career, he apparently received the ultimate tip, and went after it with everything he had and quite a bit that he didn't have. The company in question, named Xtra, was in the business of leasing piggyback containers to railroads, but for the go-go investor, the details of what a company actually makes, what services it performs, are irrelevant to the dream symbolized by its stock. On April 4, 1966, Marcus reached for that banal dream: he bought one thousand shares of Xtra, at about $96 a share. Within a week, the stock jumped ten points, and so Marcus, having made a fast $10,000, went all the way; he took another thousand shares, this time at about $106 a share. He did not, to be sure, have the more than $200,000 needed to pay in full for these purchases, but he did have credit with a finance company. At an interest rate of one percent a month, Koenig & Co. laid out eighty percent of the cost of the stock—around $160,000. Marcus's account at the time held $43,000, which went toward the remaining twenty percent. Koenig kept the stock as collateral. And then, that cruel April, as though the gods of the American Stock Exchange had nothing better to do than play jokes on James Marcus, Xtra began a precipitous drop. By the end of the month, it was down to the low eighties and getting lower; by fall, it would be hovering shakily at around $40 a share. There went Marcus's millions.

As the value of the shares fell, his friends at Koenig & Co. began pressing him for cash to keep up the value of his collateral, with the regrettable but businesslike alternative that he would otherwise be sold out. Marcus had no resources of his own and no means of raising on short notice the thousands required as the stock kept slipping and the interest charges, of about $1,600 a month, kept adding up; he did borrow from relatives, friends, and friends of his wife, but the sums proved insufficient, and his relations with his father-in-law were not such as to encourage him to seek assistance in that direction. So he turned to his new, special friend, Herb Itkin.

T W O

The Informer

*"I lived a very peculiar life
in the last few years. . . ."*
HERBERT ITKIN

IN many ages and varied climes, the legal profession has
found room for men whose careers consist of skirting,
manipulating, and torturing the law. Some spend their
lives in offices, more or less well appointed, pondering how
the letter of a provision of the tax code may be twisted to
subvert the code's spirit. Others take the courtroom for
their stage and there, on any weekday afternoon, they will
grind out a tear for any Mafioso who can meet their fee.
Whatever our reservations as to their callings, these young
men on the make and middle-aged men grown sanctimoni-
ous are part of our system; they are the testers of the law
—devil's advocates perhaps, but advocates withal.

No such plea can be advanced on behalf of Herbert Itkin. Like some of his more legitimate professional kin, he
practiced a law that was all fancy deals and contortionist
logic—but he went further, past the hazy fringes of legal-
ity, into the bush where the lawyer does not merely stand
between his client and society but becomes part of the
criminal tribe. And then moved yet further on, past another boundary, into the fantastic jungle of the police informer. Itkin's life is not an open book—pages are missing,

whole chapters are scratched out, many paragraphs have been edited; yet, from the day of his emergence as a key mover in the Marcus scandal, he has been identifiable as a rogue lawyer. But one whose vision would always exceed his reach. So extravagant was his conception of himself, so tirelessly perverse his efforts to realize that conception, that he sometimes seemed a figure out of another age. "When M. Talleyrand is not conspiring," observed Chateaubriand, "he traffics." When Itkin was not trafficking, he conspired. Cursed with a hungering after conspiracy that might have been satisfied in an eighteenth-century court but not in a twentieth-century courtroom, he made a bizarre career for himself that would bring ruin to a group of foolish, cynical, and grasping men. If our story were closer to tragedy than to farce, if only it had an Othello in it, then Herbert Itkin would be our Iago.

Itkin carried the burden of a second-generation Depression youth. Born in Jamaica, Long Island, in 1926, and raised in Brooklyn, he was, as the phrase goes, a product of the New York City school system—and of much else about New York City in the nineteen-thirties. He worked as an office boy in a law firm while going through college, attended Brooklyn Law School at night, obtained his degree in June 1953, and immediately entered the fraternity of fast-talking New York lawyers who have contributed so much to the contemporary Jewish stereotype. Forty-one years old when notoriety was showered upon him, Itkin cut a not wholly unattractive figure. He was well built— about five feet eleven inches and two hundred pounds, only beginning to run to fat—and took pride in keeping fit. A few years ago, an acquaintance reports, he won a bet with a client by doing fifty push-ups; he claims an expertise in karate. Except for its sallow complexion, his face has the homely appeal of a prize fighter's—gross-featured, big-toothed, lumpy. A remarkable spread of ear, deep-socketed eyes, fat lips, a big round chin—not the face of a matinee idol, yet agreeable enough; until one notices the mouth's readiness to compress into a sneer, the quick, mistrustful shift of the eyes—and one is prepared for the details of his career.

In the years before his sudden fame, Itkin carried on his unusual practice from a room in a set of shared offices on the fourteenth floor of 300 Madison Avenue, modest housing for a man whose operations touched fantasy—but, as Flaubert observed with regard to the operations of M. Dambreuse, great banquets are prepared in gloomy kitchens. Itkin's more conventional cases fell into the "personal injury" or "negligence" category—not the most elegant of legal callings. But even here, in a line of work distinguished by imaginary whiplash and improbable settlements, Itkin added a degrading touch of his own. He set up in business in 1957 by helping himself to the files of accident cases of the law firm where he had been working, and in a number of instances he collected on accident claims and then did not turn the money over to his clients —most of whom had been sent to him by a railway union for which he had performed some service. To go to Counselor Itkin for aid was to invite catastrophe. As trustee for a small estate, set aside to insure the welfare and education of an infant, he dissipated the savings in a chancy investment. The money from another trust he simply transferred to his own account.

Investing other people's money in unwholesome ventures took up more of Itkin's energies than the conventional practice of law. He seems to have gone through around $100,000 belonging to his mother-in-law. One of his early promotions involved drilling for gas in the Catskills. By the end of 1963, he concedes, he was "doing very little legal work." He was on to more exotic lines, pursuing wealth in Central America. Although his commercial connections in that part of the world remain elusive, they seem to have had to do with unsettled political conditions in Haiti and the Dominican Republic. From 1963 to 1964 he was registered with the Justice Department as a foreign agent in behalf of interests in both those lands, representing, on paper at least, an exile group known as the Provisional Government of the Republic of Haiti, based in San Juan, Puerto Rico; the Ministry of Education of the Dominican Republic; and the Dominican Ambassador to the United States. He also represented himself as attorney for Westrade, Inc., a Coral Gables, Florida, outfit which purportedly was to play a role in an effort by the Dominican Republic government to float a bond issue of $35 million. It is understood, too, that Itkin had something to do with an unsuccessful attempt in 1963 to invade Haiti from the Dominican Republic and depose the tyrant Duvalier. His interest in this enterprise was connected with the possibility of obtaining lucrative contracts in the event that Papa Doc fell and democracy triumphed.

These dashing activities, like his later activities inside the Dominican Republic around the time of the 1965 civil war, may have been sponsored, to some extent, by the Central Intelligence Agency. Itkin claims to have been recruited personally in the mid-fifties by C.I.A. Director Allen Dulles, on the recommendation of Senator Joseph

23

R. McCarthy, to whom he says he sent information about "crucial areas of the Far East" obtained on trips for the law firm he was connected with at the time. Later, when his area of interest shifted to Central America, he says that he found Mafiosi everywhere. They showered attentions upon him because "in their eyes I was a scheming lawyer." He became a "money-mover" for them. He claims to have remained a salaried C.I.A. "illegal" through 1967, code name "Portio."

The C.I.A. is famous for its policy of not acknowledging its agents or, indeed, that it has any agents—and certainly none of the Herbert Itkin stripe. Although constrained about public statements, government officials are nevertheless quite eager to give their side of the story in private —so long as it is reported without attribution. C.I.A. spokesmen have let it be known that Itkin's account of his relationship with the agency goes far beyond anything in their records. By their unattributable account, Itkin first came to the attention of a C.I.A. "intelligence source" in New York City in the spring of 1962. The C.I.A. man, a lawyer who had private business dealings with Itkin, responded to his tales of adventures in Haiti and the Dominican Republic and encouraged him to look into things down there. It was a rather casual association, Washington officials insist, which lasted for only about a year and from which Itkin derived no income. Indeed, he is reported to have complained that the C.I.A. still owes him about $90,-000 for out-of-pocket expenses.

It's all quite secret, but we do know that Itkin made a score of trips to the Dominican Republic, using various cover stories to conceal his political role, insofar as it existed, and attended the inauguration of President Joaquin

Balaguer in the summer of 1966 as a guest of "Tony" Imbert, the Dominican general-politician who had participated in the assassination of dictator Trujillo and was enjoying a rapport with American emissaries in the maneuverings for power which ensued. Itkin took along to the inauguration his new friend James Marcus.

Just what services Itkin performed for the U.S. government or for the people of Central America during this time remain locked in the files of the Central Intelligence Agency. For a man of Itkin's propensities, the genial corruptibility of officials in the Southern Hemisphere can only have been warming. He soon took to soliciting businessmen in America to "invest" in El Dorado. The solicitations were directed mainly at persons who had already gotten entangled with him in sticky domestic deals; after the blooming of his friendship with Commissioner Marcus, any contractor who came around seeking municipal favors could count on being offered an opportunity for remarkable profits in the Dominican Republic. A few hopeful businessmen are known to have put some thousands of dollars into his hands for investment purposes; there is no record of anyone ever seeing a penny of profit.

All of the preceding, however, falls into the category of avocation. Itkin's main line of work during the nineteen-sixties was as a most untypical sort of "labor lawyer." (One labor lawyer writes: "Though I practiced in labor law in New York for more than eight years, and though I believed during that time that I knew or had heard of substantially all the active labor lawyers in New York, I was quite surprised to learn, when the scandal broke in the press, that Itkin was a 'labor lawyer.' I have never run across him or heard his name used with relation to the New York labor law bar.") If he was not widely known among members of the city's labor bar, that was probably due to the special nature of his specialty. He served as a conduit for the passage of bribes from needy businessmen to racketeers and accessible union officials who would then arrange for large and shakily secured mortgage loans to the businessmen out of union funds. "We couldn't say no to the hoods," explains Itkin—the "we" taking in the U.S. government. "We were using them in C.I.A. activities." In these cases, Itkin endeavored to keep one and a half to two percent of the amount of the mortgage for himself. "He was really making it in 1961 and 1962," recalls his first wife. "He would bring home stacks of bills and he would give me half and say, 'This is for you. Put it in the safety-deposit box'." At one time, she reports, there was $100,000 in that box. (On the occasion of his wife's birthday in 1962, Itkin presented her with a Macy's shopping bag filled with $25,000 in five-dollar bills.)

The greater part of the many billions of dollars now invested in private pension and welfare plans for the nation's workers is, we may presume, in honest hands, but government regulation in the area is distinguished by its loopholes. Through these have leaped such labor irregulars as Herbert Itkin. In most cases, his deals were arranged with the International Brotherhood of Teamsters Central States Pension and Welfare Fund, whose reputation for gaminess is uncontested. It is a sign of our ethical advance over the time of Boss Tweed that bribes and payoffs can no longer be handled directly by the principals themselves but require an attorney-intermediary to camouflage the arrangements with make-believe escrow accounts. According to one energetic New York criminal lawyer, a number of whose clients have Mafia connections, it is not uncommon for a racketeer to feel out an attorney to see if he might prove useful in one's "business" affairs. "All of us are susceptible to corruption," Itkin muses. "These people look for the human weakness in all of us." The prudent lawyer will allow such overtures to pass unacknowledged. Itkin responded to them—indeed, he seems to have sought them out—and became a professional go-between.

He owed his start in the mortgage-procuring trade to James (Jimmy Doyle) Plumeri, a "captain" in the Mafia family of the late Thomas (Three-Finger Brown) Lucchese, and a specialist in "handling" unions. In the spring of 1961, Plumeri, with whom Itkin had collaborated on some small deals, told him: "Herb, we aren't making any money on all of this nonsense that we are getting involved in, but I have a way to make some big money. I control a group in the Teamsters Union, and I can get Teamsters mortgages. All I want you to do is get some people who can't get mortgages elsewhere, and as long as they are willing to pay a lot of green, bring them to somebody, and we will get you the Teamster mortgage, and we can all make a bundle of money."

In 1967 Itkin was able to say, with some basis, "I am almost a Mafioso myself. I have been with them a long, long time." Now and then he found a chance to mix his politics with his profession, as when he obtained an introduction from a Haitian political exile to a Haitian-born, bankruptcy-destined furniture exporter; no sooner had they met than Itkin held out the possibility of a loan from the Teamsters.

Itkin's role as a procurer of mortgage loans and bribes

has been opened to our inspection by the Justice Department, which, relying on his testimony, has brought charges against a number of his former collaborators. The first of the cases to reach the courts, in the spring of 1969, involved such practiced arrangers as Plumeri; Samuel Berger, a discredited former official of a local of the International Ladies Garment Workers Union; and Frank Zulferino, president of Local 10 of the International Brotherhood of Production, Maintenance and Operating Employees. A glance at Itkin's part in this rather tortuous conspiracy will help to make clear the niche he had found for himself in those shadowy precincts where businessmen, union officials, gangsters, and their assorted counselors meet.

By 1964 Itkin had a reputation as a man with connections who, for a price, could obtain a mortgage—"People only came to me when they couldn't get it anywhere else and they wanted more money than they were entitled to." Thrashing about in this category in 1964 was a Cleveland businessman named Shiah Arsham, a manufacturer of cashmere sweaters who was desperate for cash to pay off factors on short-term loans. He needed a lot of money, and through a New York lawyer with connections, he was attempting to get a mortgage loan of $1.5 million on his business property. He encountered difficulty at ordinary banks and other lending institutions, which did not consider his property to be adequate security for so large a loan. At a generous estimate, it was worth under $500,000. As luck would have it, his lawyer, a Scarsdale man, had some business dealings in Westchester County with a young attorney who was close to Itkin and would soon share office space with him. Arsham's lawyer spoke of his client's need; the young attorney spoke of his friend's specialty; in May 1964, negotiations began. (The number of attorneys required in such arrangements seems to support the judgment of the chronicler of New York City corruption in the thirties who observed that there are obviously too many lawyers around for them all to be engaged in honest activity.) Itkin, asked for "ten percent of the mortgage amount, seven percent by check, three percent by green—and two percent up front." Itkin defines his terms: "Well, 'green' is cash that is used under the table for payoffs. There is no record either way of the money being transferred, and so it is handed from one person to another and used for a payoff and there would never be a record of it. . . . 'Two percent up front' is, as we use it in the deals, money that we get ahead of time to pay off, because if you want these deals you have to give them money in advance. And so we call it 'up front.' In other words, before we get a mortgage, we have to make payoffs."

Before the distraught Arsham at last obtained his loan, payoffs amounting to at least $150,000 had to be made to more than a half dozen interested parties. Itkin seems to have gotten little of it. The distribution process had a Byzantine quality sufficient to discourage detailed analysis; it is enough if we understand that everybody tried to get as much as he could as early as he could and do as little as he could for it. Nor need we pause over the bickering, the mutual recriminations, the outright insults, and the veiled threats that seem to be endemic to such conspiracies, as we concentrate on Itkin's particular function. The kind of talents he showed in this deal would serve as credentials in his later relationship with James Marcus *et al.*

After being promised $20,000 in "up-front money," Itkin went to James Plumeri, the silent partner and sometime client with whom he had arranged other mortgages—"my rabbi"—and they agreed to try to get the loan from a local of the Furriers Union. While Itkin handled relations with the needy borrower, Plumeri, the veteran Mafia labor specialist and convicted extortionist, was to put in the fix with the union. But the deal began to founder as weeks passed and Arsham, who raised $20,000 for Itkin by mortgaging his home, was unable to get an appraisal of his company's property that was sufficiently overstated to serve as paper security for a $1.5 million loan. By July, Plumeri, who had only been given $500 so far, was in ill humor. He told Itkin to "straighten up" and get the appraisal: "You are embarrassing me with the people."

In August, with the appraisal still not forthcoming, Itkin approached another union man, Frank Zulferino, president of Local 10 of the Production, Maintenance and Operating Employees, which carried Itkin on its books as an attorney on condition that he kick back half of his salary to the union officers. Zulferino was willing to cooperate, for two percent of the loan. But his problem was that his union's welfare fund had in it at the time only about $50,000, not a dime of which he was willing to see loaned out to a client of Herbert Itkin. All he could supply was a letter expressing his union's intention to loan Arsham's company $1.2 million, which Arsham's lawyer would then attempt to fob off on a bank, as security for a loan which everyone hoped would keep his client afloat until the big mortgage loan came through. As Itkin summarized the scheme for Arsham's lawyer: "I have a very small union [Local 10]. They haven't got anything, but they will give you what purports to be a letter of commitment. You got to give them a letter back saying you are not going to use it at all. What you do in between is up to you, but you can take this to a bank and try and get a bank to lend you money against it, and that will buy time and save Shi [Arsham] from this foreclosure he's screaming about."

Negotiations between Zulferino and Arsham's lawyer, conducted through Itkin, hobbled on for weeks. Arsham needed a firmly stated commitment of a loan from Zulferino. Zulferino would give only a loosely stated commitment, and demanded a letter in return to the effect that Arsham would never actually trouble Local 10 for the cash. Zulferino kept dunning Itkin for more money; Arsham kept pleading financial distress. In a short time the two sides completely mistrusted one another, and everybody had it in for middleman Itkin, who began to feel that he was "too middled."

One aspect of Plumeri's usefulness in Itkin's work was demonstrated in the fall, when Zulferino, who had up to that point received $9,500, continued to press for more. Itkin persuaded Plumeri "to have a sit down" with Zulferino. They sat down, Zulferino most reluctantly, and Plumeri told him: "A lot of people have to get paid here, Frankie, and you are getting too smart." Zulferino capitulated at once but, out of Plumeri's hearing, warned Itkin: "I'll get even with you." There we have the neighborhood bully Zulferino put in place by Plumeri, big brother of the block's little wiseacre, Herbie Itkin.

Itkin assisted the manufacturer with his immediate needs by getting him loans of $60,000 from two unions— Local 10 (Zulferino, typically, promised $25,000 and delivered $5,000) and a Teamsters local—for a ten-percent kickback. By then the manufacturer was promising pay-offs to others for a $1.5 million mortgage loan from Teamsters Union funds. This deal was being worked out through Sam Berger, assisted by an inflated appraisal of Arsham's property conjured up by an appraiser acquaintance of Arsham's lawyer. With Berger too, Plumeri had occasion to show the muscle of a Mafia lord and his importance to Itkin. At a meeting called to demand from Arsham money that Itkin-Plumeri felt was coming to them, Sam Berger pointed out that it was he, Berger, who was finally getting the Teamsters mortgage. Whereupon Plumeri told Arsham: "Get out of here," and then turned on Berger: "Sam, do you want to say that again to me? You may have gotten it [the loan]. Do you want me to stop it? I'll stop it today." Berger retreated, much like Zulferino under a similar reprimand: "No, Jimmy, I didn't mean it that way." Plumeri said: "Don't tell me what you meant, and don't you ever talk to me like that again, because the next time will be the last time you ever do that, Sam." Sam said he was very sorry.

In time Arsham went bankrupt and was unable to repay his $1.5 million loan from the Teamsters Union pension fund, but by then Arsham's lawyer, fund officers, and go-betweens like Berger had already divided Arsham's $150,-000. Nothing was lost but the savings of union members. For his efforts in these frustrating negotiations, Itkin collected $30,000, of which he claims to have given various co-conspirators $23,000. His admitted net of $7,000 was disappointing, but the deal was only one of a number in which he participated in the mid-sixties—in behalf, he avows, of the Federal Bureau of Investigation.

In March 1962 Congress passed a bill aimed at just the

kind of union-welfare-fund kickbacks to which Itkin was a party. Itkin says: "I hadn't fully understood the involvement in this particular deal when we first started. Certainly, by June, I saw it as a horrendous fraud in my own mind, and at that point it became a lot more serious and a lot more violation to the Teamster members, and I hadn't realized this before. So it became a much more serious crime in my eyes. Even though I was working with another agency [presumably, the C.I.A.] and there was a reason I got involved in it, I felt at this time I had to go to the F.B.I. because this was the very crucial thing that both Attorney General Kennedy and the F.B.I. were interested in stopping, the fraud upon the welfare unions of the working people."

Perhaps Itkin was beginning to feel intimations of mortality around that time and thought of the F.B.I. as a kind of insurance firm. J. Edgar Hoover, after all, might protect one from the vengeance of the lawless as well as from the retribution of the law. "I was in with the hoods," says Itkin. "What a shot! Who else was going to take the chance?" And so in March 1963 he was passed along to the F.B.I. by the C.I.A., rather as sportive aristocrats once traded mistresses, and became a "voluntary federal informant," which the F.B.I. defines as "an individual, a citizen, who offers to furnish us information on a confidential basis, with no promise of a reward of any type."

Policemen do not have much choice in selecting informers, and without informers the fields of graft and bribery would remain virtually impregnable. So we rely for our civic defense on creatures whom we would not ask into our homes without first locking up the silver. As a federal prosecutor was to observe, when you want information on conditions in a cesspool, you do not send an angel down for it. And Itkin himself asks: "If I had been clean and pure, do you think those characters would have done business with me?" However it began, Itkin's relationship with the F.B.I. was star-crossed. He could dream of himself riding a pirate ship, sinking it with all hands save one, and walking to safety upon the waves to the general acclaim. He derived a sustaining sense of heroics as well as a mundane security from the connection; he even left off paying income taxes. The Justice Department, for its part, would obtain several firm cases and convictions of racketeers, union and secular, including, if Itkin is to be believed, the memorable Jimmy Hoffa.

Finding himself pressed, in trial after trial, as to his relationship with the F.B.I., Itkin settled upon the following explanation: "I was asked in March 1963 to infiltrate organizations in which the F.B.I. was interested. As it gradually developed, I took on my own initiative, and not necessarily with their wishes, what I felt was necessary to complete my infiltration. And throughout the years, there have been times when I have lied to the F.B.I.—or I don't know honestly in my heart that each particular act I was doing was not calculated to gain a little more money for me to swing. I felt in my heart that I would give all the evidence at a later date, though some of the things I didn't tell them. And, to be completely honest, it was for somebody else to judge what my intent was."

Such was the delicacy of his relationship with the F.B.I. that during their five years together he was able to collect tens of thousands of tax-free dollars from illicit operations. He relayed "just highlights" of his activities. The deals he reported, he reported after the fact; he elaborated upon the parts that others played, but scanted his own contribution. No one can remember him ever giving up any of his share of the payoff money; the closest he came was the time he handed over to his F.B.I. contact the wrappers from two piles of bills. Generally, reports the contact, he "told me about these deals after they were completed and he had disbursed the proceeds." The F.B.I., which acknowledges giving him only a few thousand dollars for expenses, accepted what he chose to tell.

So happy a resolution between the appetites of the body and the needs of the spirit is not given to many men. A couple of times a week Itkin, voluntary unpaid informer #3936C, code name "Mr. Jerry," would make partial confession to an F.B.I. agent. "We met in a restaurant," reports the agent, "public places generally, for short periods of time, generally. He was constantly on the move. He was meeting so many people and dealing with so many people." With no injunction to do penance, lawyer Itkin would at once return to his trade. Not, we may be sure, without a sense of honor. Asked whether, in setting up escrow accounts for loan-seeking businessmen and then using the funds therein as bribes to union functionaries, he was not violating his trust as an attorney, Itkin replies in the negative on the grounds that the escrow accounts were fraudulent to begin with and he was only doing what was expected when he milked them. Asked how he could reconcile his attachment to the F.B.I. with the fact that he profited from the criminal conspiracies he had undertaken to wipe out, he replies: "I had to live and I had to further my infiltration. . . . Either you go to the Copa with them [Mafiosi] and spend money or they won't go along with you." In his heart Itkin knew he was doing right: "I felt in my heart that every bit of information that I finally accumulated I would eventually turn over to the F.B.I."

It is not impossible that he actually believed something like this at least for some part of the time. Honesty was constitutionally out of the question for Itkin—his first wife, perhaps in an apocryphal mood, claims he even lied to his psychiatrist, "at forty dollars an hour"—but so devious were his inclinations that he could not find a straight career even in crooked work. His shrewdness took the form of undermining every confidence, betraying every trust. As a journalist of Boss Tweed's day described the Ring's Slippery Dick Connolly, "He has not an honest instinct in his nature. . . . He was an uncertain friend and a treacherous ally. No man gave promises or broke them with less compunction." It is not uncommon for a man who deludes everyone else to delude himself as well. After surfacing in 1968, Itkin had an interview with representatives from a New York literary agency, whom he regaled with his idea for a TV series based on his career. "He seemed to want a weekly show on NBC," one of the agents concluded, "with Herbie Itkin played by a gentile actor." As the name of the hero, he seems to have favored "Bret."

Although Itkin when pinned down turns rather lugubrious, his active years were lively enough. He flew about the world a great deal, ostensibly in the service of his country. At one period he had himself driven around in a chauffered limousine. He entertained attractive girls at fancy nightclubs—a taste that may be connected to his divorce and quick remarriage in 1963—and he seems to have whispered to his companions of some secret work he was doing for the government. His first wife says he also told his fellow commuters of his undercover connections.

He protests: "I never blew my cover at all," and attributes such slanders to his former wife's insecurity and antagonism. He says it was she who threatened to expose his F.B.I. connection as a means of blackmailing him. He says that she has not been able to forgive him for having the higher IQ.

Itkin conspired endlessly, shifting roles as required, dropping hints that he was more than he seemed, and playing out a low tale of high intrigue. But it was an expensive way of life, particularly after the divorce that took him from the Long Island suburbs to an apartment on Greenwich Avenue, in Manhattan, and entailed a sizable lump-sum settlement as well as continuing payments to his former wife and their four children of $350 a week, which he did not invariably meet on time. (Itkin charges that his first wife not only helped herself to $45,000 in their bank accounts but took from a safe deposit box $50,000 which had been left with him to be passed along as payoff money upon the completion of a pending deal. The former Mrs. Itkin says that *he* took the money from the box for one of his deals and never returned it.) From Itkin's explanations of his financial problems, it appears that he was constantly falling prey to unscrupulous persons: associates kept cheating him. More than once, he claims, he had the disillusioning experience of collecting a bribe from a businessman and conveying a part of it to union racketeers only to have the latter renege on the deal. He claims further that he then drew checks to repay the businessman, in good faith that the racketeers would repay him. One must accept this story, if one accepts it at all, on similar good faith—for repaying money was not an automatic gesture with Itkin, as an Arizona businessman discovered in 1964

37

when he did not get the mortgage loan for which he had paid the lawyer, and did not get back his $15,000 in front money. Itkin lays the blame for this oversight on an associate.

Whether the sums illicitly collected were spent on good works or in nightclubs, given to his family, repaid to accomplices, or shipped to a numbered account in Switzerland, we cannot be certain. But by 1965 Itkin had built up a company of forty or fifty creditors, from relatives to racketeers, one or more of whom dunned him daily.* In January of that year, his bank account was cancelled, as a result of his having written, by his own estimate, "many, many" bad checks, perhaps a hundred of them. He opened another account at another bank, and early in 1966 was requested to leave, having bounced a check for $2,700. Rather than subject himself further to the indignities of bank managers and the impositions of creditors, he "developed an association" with a twenty-eight-year-old attorney, Charles J. Rappaport, who had been working for the firm from which Itkin was renting space. "Can I use your bank account?" he asked. The impressionable Rappaport, who, according to Itkin, was not above boasting of his own in with the smart-money crowd in Vegas, readily agreed. The association was formed. Two years later, in commemoration of this courtesy, Itkin would do his best to have Rappaport sent to jail.

As it happened, one of the court reporters at the trial in

* Hardly had it been announced that I had interviewed Herbert Itkin, for purposes of this book, when I received a court order, obtained by an alert lawyer, advising that "any and all sums of money due and owing to HERBERT ITKIN by virtue of the publication of 'A Percentage of the Take' or otherwise" were to be held back from Itkin because he owed $16,199.25 to one set of creditors.

June 1968 where Itkin would make his public debut was a novelist, and so he naturally saw the informer as a Dostoevskyan figure who could not himself have predicted at any given moment or in any given situation what he was likely to do. There is something to this; yet the events that followed the meeting in 1965 between Herbert Itkin and James Marcus were not entirely unpredictable. To find language appropriate to this meeting, one must reach back to Gay Nineties music halls and confide that Marcus *fell into the clutches* of Itkin. One is properly offended to learn that a young thing has fallen into the clutches of a pimp, yet the question often remains: if it had not been this pimp, would it not have been another?

Marcus and Itkin came together first in the early summer of 1965, just a few weeks after John Lindsay's announcement that he was a candidate for mayor. The intermediary was Oscar A. Bloustein, one of the lawyers who shared offices with Itkin at 300 Madison Avenue. Bloustein wanted to help in the campaign but preferred to do so "behind the scenes," out of regard for the position of his brother, then a member of the city's Planning Commission. "Where do you need help?" he asked, and when Marcus mentioned union endorsements, not often bestowed on Republican candidates in New York City, Bloustein introduced him to Itkin—"I am sure he can help you with labor unions." It is Itkin's custom to go onto a first-name basis without preliminaries. Within ten minutes of their meeting, recalls a lawyer who was present, "Itkin acted as if he'd known Marcus for years. Something clicked between them, just as it usually did when Itkin saw somebody he thought he could use." Marcus cannot have known that

Itkin's labor connections consisted mainly of crooked, marginal, and improbable union officials.

Their friendship took fire at once. To Itkin, Marcus must have seemed a prize from the gods. The relationship with the Lodges and with the Lindsays, which Marcus took no pains to conceal, suggested large quantities of money and pull, basic ingredients in the Itkin way of life. Marcus was irresistible. But Itkin was not without appeals of his own for the neophyte politician and faltering operator. Itkin *knew* things. He knew people and powers and where the action was and where the bodies were buried and whose closets housed which skeletons. Where tips were to be had, Itkin would have them, and Marcus, the eternal outsider who wanted more than anything to be inside, had faith in tips. If Jim was the properly brought up boy with naughty inclinations, then Herbie was the street urchin who knew all the whorehouses in town. Soon, Itkin was a frequent visitor to Lindsay headquarters in the Hotel Roosevelt, and by November, election month, he and Marcus would be seeing one another almost daily. On Fridays, Marcus would pick up Itkin's children by his first wife and deliver them to their father for their weekend visit.

No sooner had John Lindsay been elected than the two young men went into business together. Says Itkin, "I felt that I had a tremendous opportunity." He reportedly had a newspaper article about mayoral assistant Marcus reprinted and mailed out to scores of people around town who might be interested to learn of this fine connection at City Hall. In time, through Marcus, Itkin would come to know almost every commissioner in the Lindsay administration—including at least one who, he claims, was not above taking a bribe. In most reports of Marcus's fall, it is taken for granted that his beating in the stock market caused him to go astray. The close connection with Itkin months before the speculation with Xtra throws doubt on that kind theory and suggests that the unhappy market experience was not the cause of the problem but only a symptom that got out of hand. Itkin tells us that he was "appalled really for Mr. Marcus," whom he felt "was innocently driven into these things in his desire to make money and make money quickly." Whatever Itkin's powers of being appalled, James Marcus did behave like a man who was at once innocent and driven, a lethal combination.

Conestoga Investments, Ltd., the first Marcus-Itkin venture, was organized in December 1965. There were four principals: Marcus, Itkin, Albert M. Greenfield, Jr.—a prominent Philadelphia real-estate broker, dabbler in Democratic politics, and son of the city's preeminent businessman—and his brother-in-law, Peter W. Littman. Greenfield had sought out Itkin in 1963, as a man with a reputation for being able to produce mortgage money through his connections with certain unions. The Philadelphia realtor thought of the New York lawyer as "a funny money man," and "a balcony financier"—that is: "When you can't get anything on the main floor, you go up to the balcony, where the interest rate is higher." In the months after their meeting, Greenfield kept in touch with Itkin, on behalf of clients who needed mortgages, but, according to Greenfield, Itkin never came through.

In 1965, Itkin told Greenfield of a lawyer friend (a classmate of his from Harvard, he explained in passing)

41

who had promising contacts within the emerging leadership of Africa's emerging states. One might reasonably assume that African statesmen would be at least as crooked as Latin American statesmen, and it was Itkin's plan to form a company that would utilize his friend's contacts in arranging investment opportunities for American capital —on the order of shipping beef from Mali, building a dam in Sierra Leone, making harbor improvements in Dakar. The company he envisioned, as James Marcus would later explain blandly, was "to be a finder of projects in various parts of the world, mainly to bring people and companies together." Itkin wanted Greenfield in on the deal because of his wealth, his reputation as a legitimate businessman, and his political connections in Washington.

Greenfield says that he resisted Itkin's overtures until the summer of 1965, when Marcus was brought forward. "I could see what Itkin was, and I wouldn't have accepted him. He couldn't sell me anything. But when he brought Marcus down, that was impressive—the special assistant to the Mayor of New York arriving here one afternoon in a chauffeur-driven limousine. I accepted Itkin on the basis of his relationship with Marcus. Marcus bridged Itkin's credibility gap."

Itkin reminisces: "Marcus was a beautiful front. He gave it a real dignity. Instead of introducing Herbie Itkin, a Jewish lawyer from New York, we could introduce James Marcus, the son-in-law of Governor Lodge."

The name Conestoga was suggested by Greenfield, who happened to reside on a street called Little Conestoga Road. Greenfield became president and chairman of the board of the new firm, and Peter Littman, his wife's twin brother, then living in Switzerland, was persuaded to take the title of treasurer and handle the European end of the business. Itkin reasoned that a British-based corporation would be less suspect in Africa than an American-based company.

Conestoga bore all the earmarks of an Itkin operation. Itkin took $3,000 from Greenfield for a business trip to Europe that he and Marcus made in 1965, and for incorporation fees. But if any business was conducted, partner Greenfield claims never to have learned of it. Itkin's lawyer friend in Dakar was asked to represent Conestoga in Africa, but he later told a reporter, "They never got very specific. They never came up with anything for me to do." Greenfield says that through his Washington contacts he helped arrange for Itkin and Marcus to pay their inaugural visit to the Dominican Republic, where they were supposed to look into the financing of an oil-storage depot, the construction of a road, and some housing. Greenfield maintains that nothing came of these ventures either: "They all turned out to be impossible situations."

During its short life, Conestoga Investments, Ltd., served no discernible function other than to provide Marcus-Itkin with impressive stationery for their private endeavors. In the summer of 1966, a woman in upstate New York, having seen the stationery and confirmed that the reputable Greenfield was connected with Conestoga, gave $2,500 to Marcus-Itkin in anticipation of a large mortgage loan which they promised to help her obtain on favorable terms. In October, still having gotten neither the loan nor the return of her $2,500, she complained to Greenfield. He protested his ignorance of the entire matter and attempted to reach his sometime associates in New York. They proved to be elusive, so on October 28, he says, he sent them a night letter:

It has come to my attention that you may have made statements, representations and commitments on my behalf or on behalf of Conestoga Investments, Ltd., without my knowledge or my proper authorization. Demand that you immediately cease using my name in any way as being associated with you in any business transaction. Consider all business relations between us temporarily terminated upon receipt of this telegram subject to all rights at law I may have against you.

"I'll be sorry for the day I met Itkin for the rest of my life," laments Greenfield, and he holds a grudge against John Lindsay for accepting someone like Marcus into his inner circle and so leading reputable businessmen astray.

Itkin, if one may believe him on this inconsequential point, early invested $6,000 of his second wife's money in Xtra on Marcus's promise that the stock was about to "skyrocket." When it began its descent toward the end of April 1966, and Koening & Co. pressed Marcus for more cash to keep up his margin, Marcus turned for advice to Itkin, who had become his mentor in many things. (Asked during the 1968 trial about his influence over the strayed Marcus, Itkin said modestly, "I didn't dissuade him and I didn't help him in it. He made his own steps, and he followed it all along.") Itkin's advice in 1966 was to this effect: instead of selling out and taking his loss—which at that stage would have been in the neighborhood of

$40,000, substantial but manageable—Marcus should hold on, keep faith, and borrow in prospects that "perhaps the stock will come back." Moreover, Itkin the insider would undertake to arrange the needed loan. This he would do as a sign of their abiding friendship, with the understanding that should the stock one day indeed rise, he, Itkin, would share equally in the profits. Infatuated with the prospects of Xtra, determined not to take his loss and quit, Marcus could not appreciate what he did to himself when he agreed to this course. By giving up half his profits and by committing himself to months of interest payments over and above what he was already paying to Koenig & Co., he reduced drastically the possibility that he could still, somehow, come out ahead. Itkin, for his part, could hardly come out behind. If there were a loss, Marcus would suffer the brunt of it. If there were a gain, Itkin would share as a full partner. Yet what choice did James Marcus have? Could the college dropout admit defeat again? Casting about for the money needed to keep this young partnership afloat, Itkin turned to Daniel J. Motto.

THREE

The Union Chief

"Is he going to play ball?"
DANIEL J. MOTTO, *in reference*
to James Marcus, as quoted by
HERBERT ITKIN

I T is possible that there will one day be an excellent account written of the American labor movement which does not contain the name of Daniel J. Motto. The omission will not be widely remarked; yet the Mottos of our age warrant a certain recognition. Having been drawn into the union game the way other sturdy fellows, their cousins and pals, are drawn into the garbage-hauling game, under the patronage of bigger rascals than themselves, they run their small fiefs like slum lords; their tenants get marginal benefits while they take in profits from several sides. Not quite full-time criminals, yet free of the inhibitions of honest men, they can be found on the fringes of deals, as finders, bargainers, go-betweens, doing their odd jobs for a percentage of the take.

At the age of fifty-seven, when he was arrested for his part in the Marcus-Itkin affair, Motto's face held the story of his career, the tough, soft, twisted face, the tight mouth, the slitted untrusting eyes. During World War II, he was convicted of black-market operations in gasoline-ration coupons, getting off with a suspended sentence of a year and a day and a fine of $1,000. He was a creature of rack-

, in their behalf he lent his radiant name to the exec-
utive board of the American-Italian Anti-Defamation
League, an organization established to spare the Cosa
Nostra a bad press. He complained of ulcers.

It was fated that the labor consultant Itkin and the
labor official Motto, president of Queens Local 350 of the
Bakery, Confectionary and Food International Union,
should find one another, even in so large a metropolis as
New York. They existed in the same element and operated
by the same rules. Local 350, which has about nine hundred members in bakeries around the city, was separated
from labor's mainstream some years ago, owing to its Ma-
fiosic propensities. On a recorded annual salary of $13,250,
Motto had managed to acquire a $57,000 house in Green-
wich, Connecticut, and a stable of trotters, as well as a
new-model Oldsmobile, with his initials on the license
plate. He and Itkin met, probably at a union dinner,
around 1964, and soon they were collaborating on small
pieces of business. Motto passed along clients in search of
Itkin's special services, both as negligence lawyer and as
finder of mortgage money. When one of them, dissatisfied
with the value he had received, threatened to bring proceedings against Itkin before the bar association, Itkin
prevailed on Motto to call the man off. In the trial to
come, Motto's attorney, fortified with his client's knowledge of Itkin's swindles, was able to put the informer
through a strenuous cross-examination.

In 1965 Itkin introduced Motto to Marcus, then a volunteer in the ongoing Lindsay campaign. As Marcus explains,
"There weren't many unions that were endorsing Mayor
Lindsay." The emissary of Reform was in no position to be
fastidious, and Motto had the virtue of frankness. At meet-

ings in his union office on Northern Boulevard in Long Island City, he made it redundantly clear to the neophyte campaigner, and, after November, to the neophyte administrator, that certain favors were expected. Not all of these were within Marcus's power, but he would be able to keep employed, for a time, an executive assistant in the Department of Water Supply named Charles Imperial, in whom Motto expressed a special interest. As it happened, Charles Imperial was a Democratic district leader in Queens, whereas John Lindsay, of course, was running as a Republican-Liberal. But district-level politicking in this country has always and everywhere been beyond ideology; it is a matter of jobs and contracts and useful information, of insurance policies and real-estate arrangements, and it works smoothly only as long as all participants to the action, whatever their labels, get a reasonable share of what is up for sharing. In the words of the "noted politician" quoted by Lord Bryce, ". . . there are no politics in politics." So no one took offense at the notion of the Republican administration saving the Democrat Imperial from having to make his living in the real world. What Imperial had done to merit such concern from Motto and other non-Democrats who approached Marcus on his behalf is not recorded.

The fruit of the Marcus-Itkin-Motto negotiations bloomed in October, when an organization by the name of Labor's Non-partisan League announced its support of John Lindsay. The endorsement of this shadowy body, formed in 1962 by several local union officials of Motto's caliber and centered at Motto's headquarters in Long Island City, was not of calculable value, but it was *something*. After all, Governor Nelson Rockefeller had esteemed

Motto sufficiently to attend a testimonial dinner for him in 1963, where he was honored for his work in behalf of the deaf children of Queens County. Lindsay's problem in 1965 was that the leaders of New York's Central Labor Council, grown accustomed to working with the city's Democratic machine and not in urgent quest of new brooms, had come out for reliable Abraham Beame. Therefore, any body, existent or seemingly existent, with the word "Labor" in its title was an asset to Lindsay—and this Motto supplied.

Motto was also able to supply some of the money that Marcus needed in the spring of 1966 to replenish his fast-deteriorating account with Koenig & Co. The approach was made by Itkin, Marcus's new partner in Xtra. He asked for $25,000. Motto agreed to a loan of $20,000, in words, as Itkin recalls, more or less like these: "Well, maybe I will lend you the money, but I want to know something first. Lindsay hasn't done a thing for me up to now, and I have been trying to get to see him and can't even get to see him." Motto put two conditions on his loan: a specific one—a guarantee that his friend Charlie Imperial would be kept in his job; and a general one—assurance that Marcus intended "to play ball with me."

Marcus, his native amiability enhanced by his need for cash, agreed. It was not difficult. After all, as Tocqueville noticed, "Stealing from the public purse or selling the favors of the state for money—these are matters any wretch can understand and hope to emulate in turn." One afternoon in April the three met in Motto's car at Forty-sixth Street between Fifth and Madison Avenues, where Motto was in the habit of picking up his wife, who worked in the neighborhood. There, Motto put Marcus through a brief catechism:

MOTTO: You are sure of this deal?

MARCUS: Yes, I am sure the stock will go up.

MOTTO: All right. Is it definite that you will keep Charlie Imperial on?

MARCUS: Yes.

MOTTO: Are you going to play ball with us?

MARCUS: Yes.

Even after this exemplary recitative, Motto had to be pressed to come up with the promised sum—but by May he had handed over $19,500 in two installments to Itkin and to Itkin's young helper Charles Rappaport. This counted as a loan of $20,000, the remaining $500 serving as Motto's interest, deducted in advance in the manner of lending institutions the world over. In addition, according to Itkin, Motto demanded to be shown a letter from Marcus and Itkin stating that $15,000 worth of stock was being purchased in Itkin's behalf, with the thought that the lender would share in the profits if, by some chance, the stock should go up. The terms were exceedingly generous by Motto's standards of moneylending, interest being computed at just thirteen percent per annum. Later in the year, the Marcus-Itkin combine would borrow another $5,000 from him; for this, according to Marcus, they would pay the more customary two-percent a week interest, or "vigorish" as it is known in the trade.

Motto was but one of the lenders who helped keep the commissioner afloat. Through the services of Itkin, Marcus was able to borrow at least $5,000, at the prevailing rate of 104 percent a year, from a loan shark in the fall of 1966—and feel himself fortunate since this entrepreneur was at about the same time charging 260 percent for loans to another of Itkin's associates. To take a loan under such conditions and from such sources speaks either of soaring expectations on the part of the borrower or of total despair. In the case of Marcus, the former seems belatedly to have given way to the latter. The value of Xtra kept going down, and Marcus, coached by Itkin, was running hard and losing ground fast. (One source of funds for Marcus-Itkin during this difficult time is suggested by a series of indictments for perjury brought in New York in 1969 and 1970. The owner of an office building, a real-estate operator, and an official who served as president of the city's Tax Commission for two years of the Lindsay administration were indicted for denying before a grand jury in 1968 that they were involved in a bribe passed in 1966 for the purpose of defeating or delaying the construction of a forty-story office building on Park Avenue between Forty-eighth and Forty-ninth Streets. The bribe allegedly went from the owner of an existing building nearby who did not want competition for tenants, to the real-estate operator, to the tax commissioner, to Marcus-Itkin, who, presumably, were to put in the fix with the city's Planning Commission. The Planning Commission did not approve the variance required for putting up the Park Avenue building until the summer of 1968.)

Motto was anything but coy about making use of his new debtor, but Marcus found most of his requests impossible to fulfill. He could not, for example, get a friend of Motto's promoted in the Corporation Counsel's office or get a judge in Queens reappointed, or guarantee a job to still another friend of his benefactor. Nevertheless, he tried to be obliging. In June 1966, when Motto was already dunning him for repayment of the lately loaned $20,000, he agreed to attend a convention of the regional council of the bakery-workers union. Motto was up for the presidency of the regional group, which took in locals in six Eastern states, and he thought it might make a good impression on the boys to have a pal of John Lindsay at his side. So it came to pass that on the afternoon of June 18, 1966, Mr. and Mrs. Marcus drove to Atlantic City from their summer home on Long Beach Island, and joined Mr. and Mrs. Motto at the Colony Motel. There Mrs. Motto told of her troubles in getting her daughter into a good school in Greenwich, and asked the former Lily Lodge whether she might help out. For an hour or so, Motto shepherded the Marcuses around the motel lobby, introducing the delegate bakery workers to the commissioner presumptive, and then he took his guest alone into a corner and, as was his custom, pressed him for favors. By now, in June, the main favor on Motto's mind had to do with the Jerome Park reservoir.

FOUR

The Reservoir

*"Meanwhile, our men sampled the
sludge. Analysis revealed that
it was stable, well digested, and
almost amorphous in character."*
"How to Clean a Big Reservoir,"
by James L. Marcus, in The
American City, *November 1967*

In November 1965, hard upon John Lindsay's election as
mayor, residents of the Bronx and parts of Manhattan
were annoyed to find dirt in their drinking water. Hun-
dreds of them complained to the Water Department,
which responded by flushing out the mains and attempting to introduce some water from the Catskills into an area
that is normally supplied from the Croton watershed and
reservoir. But in January 1966 the complaints began again.
The water was dirty; it smelled dirty; it tasted dirty. And
there was small comfort in the assurance that it was nonetheless not unhealthful.

What Bronxites were noticing were particles of the
sludge that had accumulated at the bottom of the city's
big Jerome Park reservoir in the northwest Bronx during
its sixty-one years of operation. High winds that winter
stirred up the waters of the reservoir, then at a low level,
sending foreign matter into the distribution system. It was
altogether appropriate that there be muck at the bottom
of the reservoir, which serves as a storage basin for water
from the Croton watershed; that is one of the reasons for
its existence. It holds the water—which would otherwise

go to waste, but may now be delivered to householders' faucets at peak need—long enough so that organic and inorganic material carried down from Croton can settle to the bottom. Leaves, dust, and soot also settle and undergo natural decomposition. Over the decades, this material, 175,000 cubic yards of it, had turned into a fluid grayish-black sludge blanket for the reservoir bottom, and bits of that blanket were finding their way into the drinking water of Bronxites.

In February 1966 the Water Department's chief engineer recommended that for the first time in its existence the reservoir be drained and the muck removed. The draining and cleaning of a reservoir that covered more than ninety-six acres, was twenty-three feet deep, and held 773 million gallons of water represented a project of considerable proportions. (It is, in fact, to the proud knowledge of the Water Department, the largest distribution reservoir in the nation to be drained, cleaned, repaired, and restored to service.) Such an undertaking was beyond the capacity of the department; a private contractor would have to be hired.

The City of New York uses three main methods for hiring contractors. By the first, a formal contract containing plans and specifications and approved by the city's Corporation Counsel is publicly advertised for bids from private firms. By the second, where the sum involved is less than $2,500, the contract is informal; several firms are invited to bid and the job goes to the low bidder. The third method, in which James Marcus would receive an education, employs an emergency contract, the job being awarded by the commissioner of a department without public advertisement—on a cost-plus basis. Where the costs of a project cannot be accurately estimated, a cost-plus arrangement obviously has a place. The rules, in the case of our reservoir, were that the contractor would be reimbursed for his costs plus ten percent for overhead. To that sum would be added ten percent on the amount up to $25,000; eight percent on the amount between $25,000 and $50,000; and six percent on everything over $50,000. The contractor who got the reservoir job maintained afterwards, when he was under some strain, that his gross profit on the entire project had come to only six percent, less than $50,000—but, in view of the scrabbling to get the job, there may be something to the explanation which Itkin claimed to have received privately from the man: "Well, cost-plus was somewheres between ten and twenty percent, depending on the amount of the contract, but the value of that contract was much greater, because these contractors used to put in extra equipment; in many of the contracts that is what they did, and this is the way they made extra money."

Ordinarily, emergency contracts are given out for relatively small jobs, such as breaks in the water main where, as Marcus explains, "the water is running all over the street and there isn't much time to have public bidding." Itkin and Marcus, as we shall see, would manage to turn such public calamities to their advantage. But the cleaning of the reservoir was something of an emergency too, since the extensive work had to be completed within a few winter months. The city was not yet out of the grip of the water shortage that had been an issue in the mayoralty campaign. The Jerome Park reservoir could not be shut down during the summer when demand for water was at its heaviest, and it had to be back in service by the spring of 1967 in order to catch the run-off from Croton. Moreover, it would have been difficult to draw up a contract for the job with suitable specifications since no one could say before the reservoir was drained how badly the concrete embankment had deteriorated or what was the state of the sluice gates, floor drains, and other control mechanisms. All that the department's engineers knew for sure was that it would be a big job, one that would cost the city between $500,000 and $1,000,000. It was an event in the history of New York's Water Department: no emergency contract in memory had come close to such a figure.

In March 1966, Acting Water Commissioner Marcus received from his engineers the recommendation that an emergency contract be issued for the cleaning and repair of the Jerome Park reservoir. Marcus seems not to have understood immediately the quality of the gift that was being handed to him. Like a freshly developing maiden, he required the attentions of new admirers before he could put a proper value on his own endowments. It is the custom for contractors' representatives to pay informal calls on friendly functionaries within the city's departments to gossip about what is up for grabs, and within a few weeks James Marcus was the most popular thing in town, courted by politicians, businessmen, and assorted emissaries whose intentions were approximately as honorable as those of Herbert Itkin. It was enough to make a fellow's head spin. In the interests of a coherent narrative, we shall leave most of these suitors to a later chapter and hold for the time being to the single great affair of the popular new commissioner's career.

In May, Itkin was visiting with his associate Motto in

Motto's office. The union man, as usual, was asking for favors and complaining that Mayor Lindsay was not giving him his due; but this time he had something more ambitious in mind than just keeping old friends off the streets. According to Itkin, he put his new request in more or less these words: "Look, I did the job. I got you the twenty thousand. Now there is a big emergency contract in the City of New York and Carl D'Angelo, Jr., is pushing me to get it for him. I would like to make sure that Jim is going to do this for us because this is our first big one and it is the biggest that was ever given out."

The Carl D'Angelo referred to was a lawyer and a close friend and confidant of Daniel Motto. In D'Angelo's uninformative phrase, the union leader had "recommended some matters to my office." D'Angelo drafted papers pertaining to his steeds, and was of assistance in other areas as well. The two went to the track together at least once a week. Motto was accustomed to dropping by the young attorney's office when in midtown and using his telephone for business dealings; he held at least one meeting there with Herbert Itkin. It was a close relationship. Motto says he had it in his mind to hire Carl D'Angelo as his union's counsel.

Events appear to have interfered with this plan, but at the time that Motto brought D'Angelo's name to Itkin's attention, the young lawyer was already working for Henry Fried, president of S. T. Grand Co., the firm that would get the Jerome Park reservoir contract. D'Angelo was hired in 1965, for a retainer of $5,000, which soon went up to $7,500. He handled odds and ends of work for Fried's companies—"leases, collections, and other small matters"—and, to judge by invitations extended and gifts

57

exchanged, he and his boss got along very well. D'Angelo has characterized their relationship as being "like father and son."

But, in fact, Carl D'Angelo's father was not Henry Fried. As Fried explains, "Carl D'Angelo happens to be the son of Armand D'Angelo"—who happens to have been water commissioner in the Wagner administration. Between 1959 and 1962, young Carl was an assistant district attorney in New York County, training ground not only for future prosecutors of criminals but for their future defenders as well. Carl, however, did not enter criminal law after leaving the district attorney's office. He found more respectable clients, like Henry Fried—the broker in this instance being his father. Now, why should a contractor who is dependent on the city for a great proportion of his business put the son of the water commissioner on his payroll? Such questions are best left unlabored. Still, here, for the charm of it, is Henry Fried's own account of how the association began:

"That was, I was at the Eden Roc Hotel in Florida and I was building a building—I should judge about twenty thousand feet—and I opened my door and, lo and behold, who was opposite, coincidental, Commissioner D'Angelo. He said to me, 'Henry, I would like to meet you for breakfast tomorrow.' And I said I would. 'What time?' Well, I think it was about eight-thirty in the morning, and we had coffee in the coffee shop. The building consisted of about twenty thousand square feet, and he said, 'I got a tenant for you. I want you to meet him. His name is Lavine.' And I met him. He was talking about a ten-year lease, and I never met Mr. Lavine, and, lo and behold, it was through the commissioner that brought this tenant to me and the lease amounted to ten thousand dollars—that is, it amounted to thirty thousand dollars a year, two thousand five hundred dollars a month, for ten years, and the net result was three hundred thousand dollars. There was no commission involved, and he said to me, 'Henry, I would appreciate it if you help my son and give him some work.' That is how he happened to get on my payroll."

An engaging recollection—not one hundred percent pure, yet not excessively compromising either. The kind of a story that men of the world, particularly if they were on a jury, might appreciate, and might even believe. The setting, Miami, not New York City. The occasion, a rental in a privately owned building, not any of the many emergency contracts which Fried's firm was awarded during the reign of Commissioner D'Angelo. The impulse, honest gratitude for a coincidental gesture of friendship, not payment for favoritism by an official. Whether one is able to credit this version of how Carl D'Angelo happened, lo and behold, to get on Henry Fried's payroll, will depend on one's preconceptions about municipal life.

Armand D'Angelo, though as innocent of technical knowledge as James Marcus, showed more advanced political skills during his years as water commissioner. Only once was he publicly charged with an "impropriety." In 1961 the State Investigations Commission released a report to the effect that in the spring of 1957 D'Angelo went to the office of his friend Sydney Baron, intimate adviser to the then ascending Tammany leader Carmine De Sapio, and was introduced by Baron to the Eastern sales representative of a Chicago firm that produced electrical fixtures. Baron wanted to be hired by the Chicago firm, and the sales representative was aware that the approval of

D'Angelo's office was required if he intended to do business with the city. As it happened, this firm did not retain Baron—and it received no city orders. Another lighting-fixtures firm did retain Baron and, according to the Investigations Commission, "suddenly received its first city contracts, running to more than a quarter of a million dollars in one year." Two years later, according to the commission, D'Angelo persuaded an electrical contractor who did work for the city to rewire Sydney Baron's Scarsdale home at a bargain rate. D'Angelo and Baron denied with spirit that their friendship had swept them beyond the bounds of propriety, and as things go in New York, the charges, though illuminating, were not electrifying.

In the latter nineteen-fifties Carmine De Sapio was a shaper of city politics and Sydney Baron, public-relations man and political tactician, went along on his rise to power. It is understood that our political operators do not battle their way upwards on the mucky municipal slopes in order to scorn the rewards at the top. We shall meet Carmine De Sapio later in this story and come across Armand D'Angelo (who retained his post with the Wagner administration until Wagner's own departure in 1965) again, briefly but suggestively.

In time, the father-son relationship between Henry Fried and Carl D'Angelo would deteriorate, owing to a difference of memory: Fried put the blame on Carl for getting him into the clutches of Marcus-Itkin, whereas Carl—who would be described as a co-conspirator but not a defendant in the reservoir bribery case—denied knowing anything about anything.

To return to May 1966, no sooner did the hustling Itkin hear from Motto of the big emergency contract than he hustled back to Marcus. We have Itkin's version of their conversation:

"I said, 'Jim, Danny wants us to work on a big reservoir contract. I understand it is something that is going to be the biggest ever given out. Are you going to play with us?'

"And Jim said, 'How did you hear about it?'

"And I said, 'I don't know. I guess it is all over the street. The people in the know know.' "

Marcus did not miss the drift of Motto's message: "I understood him to mean that he would find a contractor or negotiate with a contractor and there would be a kick-back." Perhaps it can be taken as a sign of residual grace that Marcus had not brought the emergency contract to Itkin's attention during the preceding weeks, and that even now he sought to hedge, although escape was out of the question for him. "I just heard about it myself," he protested, feebly and untruthfully. Then, according to Itkin, he added: "Let us not push too hard. Danny waited on the money. Let us wait a little on this."

But Itkin was nothing if not a hard pusher: "I don't know what good that is going to do us. Do you want to play ball with him or not?"

They talked, and whatever qualms or hopes of redemption Marcus may have had fell away. Inevitably, he said, "Yes, I will."

FIVE

The Racketeer

"I had Tony with me."
HERBERT ITKIN

IN May 1966, in the very first of their many conversations about the Jerome Park reservoir, Daniel Motto notified Itkin that he was planning to introduce him to "someone higher up" who would handle the deal. Itkin passed on this news to Marcus, and neither partner seems to have wondered why, considering that Motto was on such friendly terms with Carl D'Angelo, it should have been necessary to draw in still another accomplice. Marcus was not burdened with an inquiring nature, and Itkin had apparently had some experience over the years with the etiquette of Mafiadom: "The rule of the Mafia is that only certain people can be the corrupters—a Costello, a Luciano."

The fact was that Daniel Motto, despite his fine house, his trotters, and his political connections in Queens, was a small star in the Cosa Nostra universe. No *capo* he; not even a *subcapo;* not even a *caporegime.* His position relative to the dominant Mafia families was something of an in-law. He could arrange a brokerage fee on a union insurance plan, steer a client to an Itkin, make a two-percent-a-week loan, put in a good word for a pal in the municipal employ—but when it came to a serious swindle, he would defer to his betters. Motto's particular mover was Antonio (Tony Ducks) Corallo. Despite a mythology which pictures the Mafia as a centralized bureaucracy of crime, its politics owe less to Rome than to Florence. Friends and cousins and sons-in-law move in on one another as opportunity permits, make alliances and ignore them, take sides in feuds, cultivate old grudges—that is, they conduct themselves more like kinsmen than like statesmen. We may think of Daniel Motto as a small city-state existing by the grace of Tony Ducks.

Known to some of his associates as "The Doctor" and described by one student of Cosa Nostra affairs as "a loan shark's loan shark," Corallo had a considerable reputation in the Motto-Itkin circle and beyond. He is fifty-three years old when he enters our story, and his life's progress can be measured by his record of convictions. He served time in his youth for trafficking in narcotics and in his maturity for attempting to bribe a judge in a bankruptcy proceeding. Depending on the story one prefers, the sobriquet "Tony Ducks" commemorated his escape from an attempted assassination or from merited convictions. Such was his distinction by January 1967 that he was ejected from England by Scotland Yard on the basis of reputation alone shortly after his arrival in the company of his new friend, Herbie Itkin, and a reputed strong-arm type named Tommy Mancuso, the three of them apparently drawn to those shores by the opportunities inherent in legalized gambling. (Itkin politely returned home with Corallo but took the next plane back across the Atlantic—on behalf of the C.I.A., he contends: "I was there to find out about Mafia infiltration into England.") The advancement of a

Corallo from dope pusher to judge briber is yet further evidence of the openness of American society. Like lawyer Itkin, racketeer Corallo specialized in labor. The latter's influence within several Teamster locals was broadcast to the nation in 1961 by a U.S. Senate committee investigating organized crime, and it was understood by students of the matter that he was a preeminent candidate for leadership of the large and vigorous New York "family" left without a head by the death in 1967 of Thomas (Three-Finger Brown) Lucchese. (According to the F.B.I., Corallo, following a pattern cut by Lucchese, had his eye on setting up non-union garment factories in Florida.) The denouement of the Marcus-Itkin affair would get in the way of this promotion.

The entrance of Corallo, a short, broad man thickened through the middle by years of good eating and groomed from cuticles to eyebrows, brought a serious tone to the reservoir negotiations. Payoffs, after all, have a slippery quality; nothing can be put in writing, and one can hardly hope to collect a bribe by recourse to a civil suit. We have already had occasion to admire Jimmy Plumeri's ability to keep order among rascals. The Corallos and Plumeris provide stability for a society outside the law; their reputations exude a glow of security over any operation, and all parties may proceed in orderly fashion. Being above the lowest levels of crookedness, they can be looked to for rough justice by conspirators who have not had an opportunity to get to know and trust one another—or may have had too good an opportunity to learn how far each might be trusted.

The haziness surrounding Corallo's line of work calls to

mind Robert Warshow's description of the movie gangster as "the man of the city, with the city's language and knowledge, with its queer and dishonest skills and its terrible daring. . . . The gangster's activity is actually a form of rational enterprise, involving fairly definite goals and various techniques for achieving them. But this rationality is usually no more than vague background; we know, perhaps, that the gangster sells liquor or that he operates a numbers racket; often we are not given even that much information. So his activity becomes a kind of pure criminality: he hurts people." They are big men, the Corallos, fabulous men; in the minds of eternal hangers-on like Motto, they glow with wealth and power and a sort of invincibility. Just as no ordinary rabbi will do to lend his seal to canned goods at Passover, so a Corallo must be called in to certify that an extraordinary fix is kosher.

Corallo's prospective share from the reservoir deal can hardly have seemed impressive in the accounts of a lord of the Mafia, but his time and attention could be considered an investment in the future of Commissioner Marcus. It was the promise, not the immediate gain, that, we may surmise, caught and held Corallo's interest. The political cast in New York had changed with Lindsay's election; there were new men on the scene who required a certain seasoning before they could be of service to veterans of the back room. From Corallo's perspective, the Jerome Park reservoir was the baptismal font of James Marcus. One can appreciate the later exasperation of an old gangster who had gotten away with so much on being brought down for failing in so little. In December 1967, as he was waiting to be indicted, the Mafia prince complained to Itkin: "What am I doing here? You know I didn't do anything. Every time I get mixed up with you guys, I get myself in trouble."

But we are still in May 1966 when Itkin had his first meeting with Antonio Corallo. Marcus had unknowingly met Corallo in December 1965 through Daniel Motto. The young man was visiting the bakery workers' leader at his office in Queens and was invited by Motto to a nearby diner for a cup of coffee. Awaiting them there was Corallo, presumably desirous of a first-hand look at the intimate of Mayor-elect Lindsay; he was introduced as Motto's cousin Tony. At their May meeting, at the Pancake House in Queens, Itkin, who knew Corallo by reputation, received a more candid introduction. Motto presented him as "the guy that's going to handle these contracts with the city with us." No matters of substance were discussed at this first meeting—but, at parting, Corallo somewhat patronizingly confirmed the fresh relationship. He said, "I'm glad you're going to work on the contracts with us." Itkin reported back to Marcus that he had met "a high guy"— which Marcus understood to mean "the top of the Mafia."

A few days later, at the diner near Motto's office, there was a more substantive meeting of Itkin, Motto, and Corallo. Up until now it had been taken for granted by the union leader, and so by Itkin, that he, Motto, would be working the reservoir deal, through his pal, Carl D'Angelo, strategically situated in the employ of S. T. Grand and in the affections of Henry Fried. But now Corallo announced that he had elected a different emissary: "Here's what we're going to do. Joe Pizzo, who is the labor-relations consultant for Henry Fried and Mackay Construction, is going to handle this for us. He's been in a lot of deals with Henry." When Corallo left, Motto introduced a theme to which he would revert constantly in the weeks ahead. He felt he had been slighted: "I could have done much better with Carl D'Angelo, Jr., and I brought this deal to us and now he's giving it to Pizzo."

As it happened, the firm of S. T. Grand, along with Mackay Trucking, Triboro Carting, and other interests of Henry Fried, had done a great deal of business for the Water Department during the Wagner decade—mainly as contractors for water mains—and was qualified to undertake the cleaning and refurbishing of the Jerome Park reservoir. Indeed, it seems to have been singularly qualified, even without whatever special services Carl D'Angelo or Joseph Pizzo might provide. Grand owned about 350 pieces of major construction equipment and had upwards of five hundred men working on jobs around town at the time that the city was seeking a firm to master the reservoir. As the judge at the trial of Henry Fried would state more than once in open court, Grand's qualifications were not at issue. The other firms that were brought to the attention of Commissioner Marcus were smaller and less experienced; in fact, they were scarcely in the running. The Water Department's acting chief engineer, unbeholden to either Carl D'Angelo or Joe Pizzo as far as is known, and surveying the project free of the political pressures that would come to bear on his chief, concluded early that "I would give the job to S. T. Grand."

Among the less certain assets of S. T. Grand and other firms wishing to do business in New York City was Joe Pizzo. For ten years he had been on retainer to a contractors' association, his function being to "take care" (Henry

Fried's phrase) of trucking-labor contracts. As the contracts involving laborers, drillers, engineers, oilers, and other groups expired each year, Pizzo would represent Fried and his peers in settling them. Pizzo, whose death in April 1968 deprives us of his personal denials of wrongdoing, was in fact a fixer, and his career throws light, and not a pleasant light, on the intertwinings of politics, business, labor, and the rackets in the City of New York. In 1950 he was Bronx County campaign chairman for Acting Mayor Vincent Impellitteri in a mayoralty race which found branches of local gangsterdom split between Impellitteri, running as an independent, and Supreme Court Justice Ferdinand Pecora, running as a Democrat, with the support of Tammany's Carmine De Sapio. In mid-campaign, Pizzo, responding to what orders or promises we can only speculate, switched sides and came out for Pecora. Impellitteri surprised the world by winning, and went on to demonstrate during his time in office that an underdog sometimes ought to be beaten, and Pizzo resumed his profession as "labor-relations consultant." The Democrats would return soon to City Hall, and he had done himself no irrevocable harm by his show of party loyalty.

Guilt by association is a treacherous tool, and never more so than when employed against a dead man. However, when one has styled himself a "labor-relations consultant" and is closely associated with major city contractors like Henry Fried, major labor racketeers like Antonio Corallo, and the Democratic Party machine, one has invited suspicion. According to Itkin, Pizzo was involved in at least one of his deals with the Mafioso James Plumeri. Henry Fried called Pizzo "a czar in the construction busi-

ness . . . when Joe Pizzo gave a command in the construction business everybody would abide by whatever he
said." Fried's recollections of his deceased associate of
twenty-five years are marked by conspicuous self-interest,
since his defense at his trial rested on the claim that the
money he paid out for the reservoir contract had in fact
been extorted from him—yet, even when discounted
somewhat, his testimony helps us to understand Pizzo's
mysterious office: "I know that Joe Pizzo, from what I
read, was connected with the Cosa Nostra. I know that he
was a muscle man. I know he wouldn't hesitate to put the
arm on an individual. I have read about various labor difficulties that he was in. I know that if he came up and gave
me a command I would have to adhere to it. Not only me,
but so far as all the contractors in our great city are concerned, they all respected Joe Pizzo, because his word, in
my law, in my book rather, was law. I can go back twenty
years ago—and I don't want to go back too far—there was
a lot of labor difficulties in New York City with engineers,
and at that time there were forty-ton cranes, sixty-ton
cranes, dumped overboard in the river at night." Fried was
careful not to charge Pizzo with any crimes in which S. T.
Grand might have been an accomplice and on which the
statute of limitations had not run out. With due charity for
the departed, the testimony goes to suggest that Pizzo, like
the estimable Corallo and others of their calling and generation, had some time since given up sheer muscle and
was pursuing his trade in a businesslike manner—his credentials a proved effectiveness at keeping peace in a vul-
nerable industry, a reputation for political connections,
and a scent of potential violence that wafted from him like

after-shave lotion. In choosing Pizzo to be the bagman for Henry Fried, Corallo did what any sensible racketeer would have done in the circumstances.

Daniel Motto, however, was not pleased. As he left the Queens diner with Itkin after hearing Corallo outline his plan of action, he was still grumbling: "This is a heck of a note. I bring in the deal, I bring Tony in, and now he is going to do it with Pizzo. I can do much better with Carl D'Angelo, Jr."

Whereupon, Itkin inquired: "Why don't you go to Tony and tell him?"

Motto answered: "You can't talk to Tony that way. When he makes up his mind, that is it."

Itkin, to whom we are indebted for the above exchange, as for most of the dialogue of Motto and Corallo, understood. When Marcus mentioned to him some weeks later that Motto was still discontented, Itkin told him: "It's not up to us who handles the negotiations." It was up to Tony.

At the diner meeting in May, Corallo asked Itkin, "How much do you want?" Itkin, relaying the question to his partner, confessed: "I don't know what the going price is. I really don't know how much to ask." And if Itkin, the professional, was puzzled on this point, what could have been expected of the amateur Marcus? The two resorted to simple arithmetic to calculate an answer for Corallo. Their partnership had debts outstanding at the time of about $75,000. Estimating that the reservoir contract would come in at around a million dollars, Marcus settled on a cut of seven and a half percent as being just enough to meet his needs. In Itkin's phrase, "seventy-five thousand dollars in green."

Itkin called Corallo, and a few days later the two of them met Pizzo at Gian Marino's restaurant on Lexington Avenue.* Pizzo, a man who could be expected to know whereof he spoke on questions of payoffs, reacted quickly to the figure of seven and a half percent: "My God, that's much too high." He did not think the matter could be arranged at that price. But Corallo, less devoted to the deal at hand than to the development of a continuing relationship with the mayor's friend, ruled: "Well, if that is what he wants, that is what he wants. Go get it." Pizzo said he was meeting one of Fried's brothers and would present the asking price.

It was now June of 1966, the beginning of a summer lull in the conspirings. Marcus and Itkin met twice more with Motto, who only reiterated his discontent at having been edged off his own turf. Again he argued, impotently before an impotent audience, that his man D'Angelo could do better with Henry Fried than Corallo's man Pizzo. It was as consolation to peevish Motto that Marcus presented himself for the appreciation of the bakery workers at the Atlantic City convention that month. At the end of June, Marcus accompanied Itkin to the Dominican Republic for the inauguration of President Balaguer. They returned home for the weekend of July 4th, and Marcus joined his family on holiday while Itkin went off on one of his mysterious journeys for most of July. The first weeks of August

---

* Just what standards Corallo and Pizzo used for their meeting places requires further study. One thing seems clear—it was not the food. In his *Guide to Dining Out in New York,* Craig Claiborne allows Gian Marino not a single star. He was offended by the heavy dousings of oil and garlic, and while conceding that the pasta dishes can be excellent, he described the bolognese sauce that accompanied the tagliarini as "pedestrian." The best thing he could find to say of the restaurant was that it is close to Bloomingdale's and Alexander's.

found Marcus vacationing in Maine, and so it was not until the middle of the month that he began to receive hints that all was not going well, that the fee he had set for his compliance might prove unrealistic.

The bad news was conveyed, not without satisfaction, by Motto. At an August meeting in a restaurant near his Long Island City office, he told Itkin and Marcus that they were asking for too much money, and took the occasion, once again, to advertise his own superiority as go-between with S. T. Grand. He claimed to have known Henry Fried for a long time—an exaggeration, at least—and expatiated on their common interest in horses. As for the payoff price, he said, "Henry Fried isn't going to go for it," and he suggested, "You guys ought to consider coming down a little in what you are asking."

James Marcus, at several removes from the site of the negotiations, did not quite. catch the drift of things. "That is what we are asking," he told Motto. "Let's see what happens."

In September the case was put to Itkin more bluntly by Motto and Corallo. They met at the Loren East Restaurant on the East Side of Manhattan, a hangout of Joe Pizzo's, and at the Pancake House in Queens. At one of these sessions, Itkin was told, "Look, fifteen percent is just too much for Henry Fried to pay, and we can't get this amount. We just can't get it." Itkin was taken aback. It had not occurred to him, nor certainly to Marcus, that their associates would tack another seven and a half percent onto *their* seven and a half percent and make a demand of Fried which even they in their hopefulness recognized was excessive. In fact, it seems not to have occurred to either Marcus or Itkin that the Corallo-Motto team planned to ask for anything above the somewhat arbitrarily set fee. When Itkin raised a mild objection, observing that it was "the commissioner" who held pride of place in their combine, Motto countered, "Listen, the guy that picks up the green should get fifteen percent for himself. And that is Pizzo."

From beginning to end, the reservoir transaction bore no trace of the vaunted Mafia efficiency or family feeling. It was unbusinesslike throughout, muddled by needless middlemen, loose agreements, looser bookkeeping, and a prevailing air of disarray. Itkin confesses that he was reluctant to bring the fifteen-percent news back to Marcus, but after a while, under Motto's naggings, he did. The report was, of course, distressing, but Marcus had the comfort of knowing there was nothing he could do about it. His investment in Xtra was showing no improvement. The price of the stock that September was at around fifty, and with the peculiar logic of the market plunger possessed of a good tip, or merely possessed, he concluded that the moment called for a fresh infusion of cash to Koenig & Co. Since purchasing the stock at its September low would reduce the average cost-per-share of his investment, he would, in Itkin's restrained estimate, "have a better chance of getting even some day." The speciousness of Marcus's reasoning, his desperate faith that he might extricate himself from his predicament by the same devices that had originally ensnared him—these were basic ingredients in his whole unhappy career. An innocence that went deeper than mere inexperience undermined his cupidity. He was willing enough to do anything, to take from anyone; but unprotected by the cynicism and low worldliness that had been bred into the bones of Corallo and Motto, he had not the means to guard himself against being taken. Perhaps it was this felt incapacity that originally led him into the arms of Herbert Itkin. Now, through Itkin, he sent a message to Corallo to the effect that he would consider coming down in price if the racketeer would advance him $10,000 so that the partnership of Marcus-Itkin might increase its purchases of Xtra. Privately, the two agreed that they would lower their asking price to five percent of the reservoir contract.

Tuesday, September 27, 1966, was an important day for James Marcus, a day of ceremony and conspiracy, when in the space of a few hours he swore allegiance to the people of New York and took part in a meeting dedicated to betraying the trust he had barely assumed. That Tuesday, at eleven o'clock in the morning, Marcus, generously described for press purposes as "a thirty-five-year-old banker and businessman," was sworn in as the city's Commissioner of the Department of Water Supply, Gas and Electricity, at an annual salary of $25,000 and perquisites. He issued a call to civic consciousness: "I hope and urge that New Yorkers will conserve water to the best of their ability." Itkin, who had spent the morning with Motto, attended the solemn event in the Board of Estimate room at City Hall. As the congratulations died away, he whispered to his friend that a meeting had been set up for that afternoon with their accomplices.

At 4 p.m., sustained by a luncheon at Longchamps with relatives and well-wishers, Marcus met Itkin at the Shelton Towers Hotel, where Itkin was living at the time, not far from the Loren East. Itkin said that he would go on ahead as a scout and directed Marcus to call him in twenty minutes for the all-clear. One would have imagined that this precaution was taken out of respect for the spotless public image of a new-made commissioner. As Itkin recalls the event, however, it was Corallo's sensibilities that were uppermost in his mind. He was not worried that Marcus might be embarrassed by being seen with Corallo, but that Corallo might be embarrassed by being seen in the company of Marcus: "Because you are never sure who Mr. Corallo is with, and he might not want the commissioner to come in if he had people that he didn't want Mr. Marcus to see or he didn't want to know that he was dealing with Mr. Marcus." Corallo wanted Marcus all to himself.

Arriving at the restaurant, where he would afterwards meet frequently with Pizzo and Corallo, Itkin found the two at a table with several other men—among whom he recognized Armand D'Angelo, the former water commissioner. D'Angelo was being loudly cursed out for his failure to perform some expected favor. When Marcus called, Itkin advised, "Jim, the coast is clear, come on over." Marcus did come over, and found Itkin waiting for him by the hatcheck booth. "There's a friend of yours in there," he said. "Armand D'Angelo."

Marcus glanced in, saw D'Angelo, and drew back. "I don't think I should go in there."

Itkin reassured him: "Don't worry. Anybody that is in there is not going to mind seeing you two together."

Still uneasy, Marcus decided to make a few phone calls in hopes that D'Angelo would take the opportunity to depart. As he was finishing his last call, D'Angelo did leave— but he made a point of stopping at the phone booth to shake Marcus's hand and wish him well. As Marcus recalls the moment, D'Angelo "said if there is anything he could do for me he would be glad to, if I had any problems with labor to let him know and that he would be glad to help, and he was generally very nice. And then he left."

Now, what lesson can a fresh-minted public official have drawn from this encounter? Coming upon his predecessor, father of Carl D'Angelo, friend of Henry Fried, in intimate converse with men whom he knew to be Mafia types with a continuing interest in the science of payoffs? What message was there for him in Itkin's observation—"Anybody that is in there is not going to mind seeing you two together"? And what meaning can Marcus have assigned to the offer of help in handling the city's *labor* problems? The kind of help, perhaps, that Joe Pizzo sold to Henry Fried? The meeting with D'Angelo cannot have been edifying for a novice in municipal affairs; rookie cops, after all, ought to be spared the sight of old-timers being entertained in the local betting parlor. Marcus can only have drawn dangerous comfort from the thought, possibly unjust to Armand D'Angelo, that the channel into which he had been directed by Itkin had been navigated by others who reached the far shore safely, indeed with honors.

At the Loren East that afternoon, Marcus and Itkin and Corallo and Pizzo (neither of the latter being known to Marcus by his full name—Corallo was "Tony Frankel," Pizzo was plain "Joe") brooded together over the difficulties of coming to an agreement with S. T. Grand. Corallo, who did the talking for his half of the combine, suggested that the other half was asking for too much money. The conversation, as received from Itkin, then went as follows:

"Jim said, 'I understand you are asking for fifteen percent. No wonder we haven't got a contract.'

"Tony said, 'Don't you think we deserve it too? We are the ones taking the risk. We are picking up the green.'

"Marcus said, 'Well, I guess it is all right, but what about the loan Herb has talked to you about?'

"Tony said, 'Well, if you come down, I think there is going to be a deal, and I will lend you the ten.'

"I think I was the one who said, 'All right, Jim, what about five percent?'

"And Jim said, 'Okay, five percent.'"

But, as Itkin soon learned, it was not okay. Marcus, having been thrown into the major leagues of corruption without benefit of a season in the minors, never quite understood the nature of the game or of the players. "I didn't know the rules," he reflected ruefully. It was all too tough for him; he would be chiseled down and chiseled down and, finally, just chiseled. His $75,000 asking price had been smoke and with it vanished his hopes for clearing away his nightmarish debts.

Corallo, a frequent visitor to Itkin's office now, dropped by a day or so after the inauguration to tell him that the deal was dead. Joe Pizzo had apparently met with Henry Fried and one of his brothers and they had turned down the ten-percent figure—five percent for Marcus-Itkin, five percent for Corallo-Pizzo-Motto. Itkin proposed calling in Motto, who had been arguing all along that he, bosom pal of Carl D'Angelo, could arrange matters better than Pizzo, with profit all around. Corallo now agreed, adding the caution that Itkin was not to say anything about the change to Joe Pizzo, and Itkin called Motto. (Asked by an attorney whether at this point he feared the wrath of Joe Pizzo, Itkin replied, "Not at all. . . . I had Tony behind me.")

Their conversation, according to Itkin, went as follows:

ITKIN: "Danny, look, you have been saying all along you can handle the contract, and you were right all along, too, because Pizzo cannot do it."

MOTTO: "Fine, but we are not going to get anywhere near the ten. We are going to get maybe five."

ITKIN: "How do you know this?"

MOTTO: "Because Carl told me Henry Fried won't pay a dime over five. He is used to paying five and that is all he is going to pay."

A few days later, in a luncheonette near where he customarily parked to pick up his wife after her day's work, Motto repeated this message at a meeting with Corallo and Itkin. He wanted a go-ahead from Corallo: "Look, Tony, I know I can get it, and there is no doubt in my mind—but I can't get more than five percent. Now, is this going to be satisfactory to the commissioner and is it going to be satisfactory to you?"

Corallo, The Doctor, replied, "If that's the best you can do, that's the best you can do, and the commissioner will just have to go along with us." For many years Corallo had made a livelihood out of knowing who would go along and under what circumstances; he needed only two conversations with Marcus to make his judgment.

Still, on receiving the dismaying news from Itkin, Marcus threatened halfheartedly to back out. But Itkin had only to remind him of Corallo's promise of $10,000 and he succumbed. He did, however, add that there was one thing he wanted understood: "I want three percent and the rest of you can share two percent." Such was the force of his personality that Itkin would wait some weeks before relaying this proviso to Corallo. At first, early in October, at the Loren East, he merely reported to Tony that Marcus had given his okay, and received for the news an envelope containing $10,000; this, together with $5,000 more from Motto, went to Koenig & Co. (In a break with ordinary business practice, Corallo's loan was apparently repaid without vigorish.)

October 1966 was another sorry month for Xtra, which was falling through the $50 range, into the forties. Koenig & Co. kept pressing for cash to sustain the Marcus-Itkin margin, and the two decided to invite Corallo to invest with them, on exceedingly inviting terms. Corallo agreed to give $10,000, to be used in buying two thousand shares of Xtra on margin. Should there be a rise, he expected a return of four dollars for every one dollar invested. Marcus explains: "Tony would loan us $10,000 and receive a four-for-one deal on the purchase. For every dollar that he put up he got four dollars' worth of stock." Later Corallo would promise Itkin: "If we make a profit, I'll share it half with you." Whether the "you" included Marcus is not clear.

Jacob Kossman, Corallo's lawyer, had some fun in his questioning of Marcus about the peculiar four-for-one $10,000 investment:

KOSSMAN: "Did he get $40,000 in cash from you?"
MARCUS: "No."
KOSSMAN: "Did he get it from Itkin?"
MARCUS: "No."
KOSSMAN: "Did he get $40,000 worth of stock?"
MARCUS: "No."
KOSSMAN: "What did he get?"
MARCUS: "He got an agreement."
KOSSMAN: "And an indictment."

Having laid down the four-for-one condition for his investment to Itkin, Corallo added one final condition: "I want to see Jim before I give the money."

The second business meeting between Corallo and Marcus took place in mid-October, soon after Motto had triumphantly notified Itkin, "You've got your deal. It is closed at five percent with Henry Fried." Marcus and Itkin drove together, in the commissioner's official car, to the Tower East Restaurant at Seventy-second Street and Third Avenue, where Itkin went inside to "see if everything is clear." Everything was not clear; the busy Corallo had some friends or associates with him, and he told Itkin to wait. This scene, of the New York City commissioner waiting in his car outside a restaurant at the pleasure of a racketeer, encapsules the Marcus-Corallo relationship. After fifteen or twenty minutes, Corallo came forth to confirm the $10,000 investment and to make the point for which Marcus had been summoned uptown: "Well, now that we have done Jerome Park, can we do some other things?"

The commissioner replied, "Yes, we can." According to Itkin, he added, "Thanks, Tony."

No sooner had Corallo made his investment than Xtra began to rise; by the end of 1966, it was in the sixties. In March 1967, with Xtra selling at around eighty, Corallo decided he wanted to get out and he collected $18,000, half the profit of his short-term gain presumably going to partner Itkin. Xtra moved steadily upward. In August 1967, the stock that had aroused so much hope in Marcus and caused him such critical disappointment was back up in the nineties. But by then, having anticipated by half a year the tide that would have brought him fortune, he had

already been forced to sell out: in November 1966 he had
to dispose of two thousand shares at slightly over $46; in
the spring of 1967, when the stock was in the eighties and
Corallo wanted his profit, he sold the remaining two thousand shares. That left Marcus about $100,000 in debt, and
as Xtra continued to rise, he might be forgiven for con-
cluding that the American Stock Exchange, like everything else he touched, was under the spell of the Mafia,
and that Al Capone was right when he observed: "Wall
Street is crooked." (By the time Marcus was brought to
trial in June 1968, Xtra had fully justified his faith; the
stock had split three for one and was listed at over $60.)

It was not until the very end of October or early in November 1966, at a meeting in the diner near Motto's office,
that Itkin mentioned to Corallo the matter of fee splitting.
Whereas Marcus had told Itkin that he expected three
percent for himself, Corallo had made it clear that the
three percent was to cover both Marcus and Itkin, with
the remaining two percent being divided between himself
and Motto. "You've got to clear this up with the commissioner," said Itkin.

Corallo replied: "Leave it alone, I'll take care of it. Just
set up a meeting in your office, and I will handle it."

Again we are indebted to Itkin's memory for a lesson in
the Corallo method of handling public officials. At a
meeting early in November, Corallo and Marcus came to
their understanding:

CORALLO: "Look, Jim, we've got a contract, right?"

MARCUS: "Right."

CORALLO: "We are going to do some work in the city,
right?"

MARCUS: "Right."

CORALLO: "Three for you, two for us, right?"

MARCUS: "Right."

As he left the meeting, Marcus told Itkin, "See, I stood up and I got my three percent."

Corallo told Itkin, "See, it's all settled. When the time comes, we'll just give you three for the two of you."

SIX

Principals and Intermediaries

*"The thing that appalled me
the most was the hard, ingrained
people who have been taking bribes
and polluting the city for years."*
HERBERT ITKIN

THE Jerome Park reservoir music suffered from an excess of themes, some in tune with the dominant Corallo-Motto-Pizzo melody, others in discordant clash. In the summer and fall of 1966, as his expectations of profit were being pushed down and still further down, Marcus found himself the object of attentions from contractors and their representatives, all of whom had had more experience than he with city affairs and most of whom seem to have received an education on the order of Mr. Jonas Chuzzlewit—which "had been conducted from his cradle on the strictest principles of the main chance. The very first word he learnt to spell was 'gain', and the second (when he got into two syllables), was 'money.'" The forms of this courtship, flattering to a young man even though he could not fail to sense that he was not truly loved for himself alone, are suggestive of the manner in which business proceeds at a certain level of municipal government.

Three main suitors, or sets of suitors, sought liaison with Marcus in 1966, the reservoir contract standing as a kind of dowry. Of S. T. Grand we have already heard something. In addition, there was the Oakhill Contracting Company, run by Ernest Muccini and son. And there was a firm called Daril, in the charge of Edward Orlando and Vincent Grillo.

Of this group, only Henry Fried, proprietor of S. T. Grand, was big-time. To intercede for him with the commissioner, he chose no less an emissary than Vincent Albano, the Manhattan Republican Party chairman and political patron of John Lindsay. (Readers who are puzzled as to how Republican bosses occupy themselves in New York when there is no John Lindsay at hand are referred to the late Democratic boss Ed Flynn's description of the Republican Party of 1914 living "from 'reform' to 'reform', its bosses keeping themselves alive during the long droughts by accepting handouts from Tammany's back door.") In the weeks preceding his inauguration, Marcus was contacted "on numerous occasions" by Albano with reference to Fried and the reservoir contract. Marcus, in the safe bureaucratic fashion which he did not always observe, suggested that Fried write him a letter, and indeed he received a communication, dated September 7, 1966, wherein were set forth the experience and resources of S. T. Grand, Inc., Henry Fried, President. But Fried was not a man to rest his hopes on a form letter. He knew and valued the uses of personal contact, and Vincent Albano obliged him in October by inviting Marcus for a drink at the Hilton Hotel, where the Republican organization was then quartered for the 1966 Rockefeller gubernatorial campaign. There, in the Bourbon Room of the Hilton, the introduction was made.

Marcus provides the gist of the conversation: "Mr. Albano said that if I could give the job of Jerome Park reservoir to Mr. Fried, he would be very appreciative. That Mr. Fried had always been a heavy contributor to the Republican Party, and any work that I could give Mr. Fried, he would be very appreciative." No money payment was alluded to at this meeting; the solicitation was political. As Marcus explains, ". . . when you get called in by the county chairman and asked to give the job to a certain company, you get the message." Marcus acted upon the message by recommending Fried and firm to other city officials.

The dropping of the name of Vincent Albano in among such names as Corallo, Motto, and Pizzo at the June 1968 trial caused agitation in the city's Republican establishment. A response was called for, and so an "informal study" was undertaken by two of Chairman Albano's more prominent peers on the G.O.P. county committee—Bruce Bromley, former judge of the State Court of Appeals and a member of the Wall Street firm of Cravath, Swaine & Moore, and Peter Megargee Brown, a lawyer with the Wall Street firm of Cadwalader, Wickersham & Taft. (The names of old-line Wall Street law partnerships seem designed not just to inspire confidence but to knock one positively flat: without them, it is doubtful that any non-paying committee in the city could ever be staffed. Only a weakness for the iconoclastic can permit one to doubt that partners in such concerns must be above the weakness of lawyers from, say, Brooklyn—yet there is something diverting about depending on men who have made their fortunes in the service of big corporations and big financial institutions to pass on the ethics of their fellow citizens, or even their fellow Republicans.)

The messrs. Bromley and Brown took four months to

examine and ponder the few lines of pertinent testimony, and then they delivered their report. They took care to note that no criminal act was involved, but concluded that "so far as considerations of propriety are involved, it seems to us unwise and probably unethical for political leaders in the position and of the stature of Mr. Albano to introduce substantial contributors or any person to government officials for the purpose of aiding the persons involved in doing business with the city or government agency. We realize that the practice is apparently widespread in both major parties and that there may be nothing inherently improper in the mere introduction. However, we believe that such communications can carry an implication of possible benefit to the government official flowing from a powerful political party. We therefore think that this imprudent practice should be stopped."

Despite a prose style that causes the teeth to grind, the observations were beyond reproach. Albano had been caught performing for a party contributor the kind of favor that political party chairmen were set on this fair earth to perform. "I never considered it wrong to introduce a businessman to a commissioner," remarks a former member of the Lindsay administration's upper echelon. Yet it came as something of a puzzle when Mayor Lindsay issued a statement commending Judge Bromley and Mr. Brown for their public service and agreeing with them as to the desirability of precluding "even the impression of impropriety or ethical compromise"—only to add: "Their finding of no wrong-doing confirms the personal and political integrity of Vincent Albano." The mayor went further: "Mr. Albano has underscored this by his progressive approach to public affairs, his complete cooperation with

Judge Bromley and Mr. Brown, and by his public endorsement of their recommendations." With a stroke of the pen, the compromised had been transformed into the occasion's guest of honor, an exemplar to us all.

Although the act of bestowing a medal on a politician for helping to lead a public official astray was unbecoming in a man of John Lindsay's quality, his predicament was not easy. Vincent Albano had sponsored him at the outset of his political career, when he ran successfully as an insurgent Republican for the congressional seat from New York's seventeenth district. "In those days," a campaign worker reminds us, "nobody else wanted to be near Lindsay." Eleven years later, after the liberal Lindsay lost his party's mayoralty nomination to a conservative from Staten Island, Vincent Albano stood by him. One does not subject such a friend, particularly when he still holds his party post, to the discourtesy of public criticism. "Vince is a good guy," says a Lindsay man, "a likable guy. He has a heart of gold. But I wouldn't make him a director of my company." New York's mayors have supped with far shadier characters than Vince Albano: as William O'Dwyer said in reference to his relations with Frank Costello, "There are things you have to do politically if you want cooperation." We may solace ourselves with the belief that at the hour of his testimonial the mayor in his heart of hearts was not cherishing Vince Albano and was perhaps even muttering an aggrieved amen to the observation of Theodore Lowi that "the perpetual bane of the reformer's existence is the ease with which the party leaders adapt new structures to old purposes."

Other New Yorkers, not inhibited by gratitude, could be harder on Albano. The Citizens Union suggested that he step aside as chairman of the County Republican Committee or be suspended pending the results of a formal investigation. *The New York Times,* ordinarily well disposed toward the mayor, now chided him for his "adroit footwork" and called Albano unfit for his post—which, considering the post, was quite insulting. And in its decision upholding the conviction of the principals in the bribe cases, the U.S. Court of Appeals went out of its way to cite Albano's role in the affair. Vincent Albano represented himself as being "highly gratified by the Bromley-Brown report" and stated that he would not again introduce businessmen to city officials.

The approach to city contracts of Edward Orlando and Vincent Grillo and their associates was not so high-powered as that of Henry Fried, yet there was method to it. For that story, we must rely on the testimony of Itkin and Marcus and charges brought by the New York district attorney. Between June and August of 1966, Vincent Grillo and William Moultray, joined in an association known as Vintray, made a deal with Itkin-Marcus by which the latter agreed to favor the former for city contracts in exchange for a five-percent kickback. Itkin's young man, Charles Rappaport, was listed as attorney to Vintray, and Gus (Buddy) Spatafora, a thirty-one-year-old Brooklyn "salesman," acted as bagman for the operation. In August, Spatafora received $10,000 from Moultray and passed it along to Itkin, who signed a promissory note payable to Grillo in thirty days if no contract was forthcoming.

Vintray having attained entree, it still remained to find a contractor who could actually perform whatever jobs Marcus might provide, since Grillo and Moultray between them could not qualify to fix a leak. The instrument chosen was the N. A. Orlando Contracting Co. of Queens, a firm of modest size ($500,000 value in 1967) which had done a score of jobs for the Water Department since 1960. In August 1966, Buddy Spatafora introduced Itkin to Edward Orlando, a vice-president of the company as well as son of its founder. According to Itkin, "He was interested in getting a contract in the Dominican Republic and contracts in the City of New York. I told him I would handle both for fees." Grillo and Orlando each gave $3,750 to Itkin as a "retainer" for his inimitable assistance.

"The day I met Vince Grillo," Orlando moaned seventeen months later, "was the saddest day of my life. We never had any dealings with Vintray before or after our joint operation." Whereas Henry Fried was an impresario of corruption, Orlando was merely a run-of-the-mill performer. If it had not been him, it would have been another. Pleading guilty to conspiracy and bribery, he presented himself as an honest businessman as the world goes, with a common, if lamentable, susceptibility to fast-talking operators-about-town: "Vintray approached us about doing work in the Dominican Republic. They were supposed to finance it through this fellow Bill Moultray. Itkin promoted the idea. I was introduced to him by these people."

Contracts turned out to be elusive in the Dominican Republic—to which Orlando, Grillo, and Moultray actually paid a visit in September 1966—but they were available in New York City. In August, Marcus asked his department's chief engineer to interview representatives of a firm soon to be known as Vintray-Orlando-Daril, Inc. (Vincent Grillo having an insatiable taste for acronyms), with a view to awarding emergency contracts on water-main breaks. Marcus attended the meeting, and it developed satisfactorily. Acting Chief Engineer Abraham Groopman explains: "Since Orlando had been doing this type of work for us before and since Orlando was going to do the repair work with his force and with his equipment, and Orlando has been the regular contractor for us, doing quite a bit of water-main work, we felt they were qualified to do emergency repair work on water mains." The Water Department officials could not figure out what function Daril was supposed to serve, since all manpower, equipment, and experience were being supplied by Orlando—but perhaps they had been around long enough to shrug away such puzzlement.

Although the original plan of the organizers of Vintray-Orlando-Daril was to buy their way into modest emergency repair jobs, they were not dead to loftier ambition. When they learned of the Jerome Park reservoir project, they determined to make a try for it. Itkin prevailed upon Marcus to invite them in to talk with his engineers, and in October 1966, at about the time that Motto was putting the final touches on his agreement with S. T. Grand, Grillo and Orlando called again at the Water Department, with a couple of associates, and again Commissioner Marcus lent his presence to the meeting. In vain. Although N. A. Orlando had proved its competence in repair work over the years, it was judged not up to the demands of cleaning a reservoir, and the commissioner was so informed by his chief engineer. (If Orlando-Grillo had been able to buy the contract to clean the reservoir, they would then have had to come to an understanding with S. T. Grand or another firm that was able actually to do the job.) Orlando went back to his emergency repair work. The records of the district attorney indicate that between December 1966 and October 1967 his firm was awarded three emergency contracts, ranging from about $16,000 to $25,000, and that Itkin received a total of $10,500—of which $4,000 was *in advance:* prompter payment than the Marcus partnership was receiving from Henry Fried during that period, as well as a much better percentage. Orlando-Grillo could not have come out of this deal very well—or if they did, then New York's emergency contracts are far more lucrative than they ought to be.

Irksome as the news of Vintray-Orlando-Daril's inadequacies must have been, Marcus seems to have taken it with at least outward indifference. "Forget about them," he told Acting Chief Engineer Groopman. "Let's call in somebody else." And he suggested somebody else—the Oakhill Contracting Company of Queens, a more substantial firm than Orlando, though considerably smaller than S. T. Grand. Some weeks earlier Marcus had been contacted by Joseph Ruggiero, chairman of the Law Committee of Vincent Albano's New York Republican Committee. Ruggiero was serving Oakhill in somewhat the same capacity in which Albano had served S. T. Grand—but there was a significant difference. After his first meeting with Ruggiero on Oakhill, in September in the Roosevelt Hotel's Rough Rider Room, Marcus assumed that an illegitimate deal was in the works. Ruggiero offered no money at this meeting or at the three other meetings they had in the ensuing weeks, but there was something in the way he said, "They are good people to do business with," that suggested a payoff to Marcus.

It was now early November, and Marcus knew that the best he could expect from S. T. Grand was three percent of the reservoir job, though he seems to have had no apprehension at that stage that even this niggardly sum would have to be shared with his partner Itkin. Pressed for cash, disappointed in his expectations, he was open to fresh overtures. So he made it a point to be present for a few minutes on November 2 when Muccini father and son came to make a show of Oakhill's competence to the Water Department. Afterwards, engineer Groopman conveyed to the commissioner the staff opinion that Oakhill was qualified to clean the Jerome Park reservoir. Within an hour (the speed with which such news spreads among interested parties within the city stands as a rebuke to U.S. postmasters), Joseph Ruggiero arrived at Marcus's office and, according to Marcus, he said, "I want you to know that if they [Oakhill] could get the Jerome Park reservoir job, there's ten percent, five for you, five for me."

(Joseph Ruggiero has denied that he made any such offer, but if we credit him rather than Marcus on this detail, we are left with the problem of explaining why, in the absence of likely gain, Marcus should suddenly have decided to renege on his arrangement with S. T. Grand. The messrs. Bromley and Brown did not feel that they were equipped to inquire into alleged violations of the law, especially since Ruggiero had resigned his post with the Republican County Committee. According to Marcus, Vincent Albano also exerted himself in behalf of Oakhill regarding other contracts.)

For Marcus the public official, to accept his own version of the incident, the relationship with Ruggiero-Muccini was scarcely more commendable than the relationship with Motto-Fried, but for Marcus the man this new liaison was as close to a show of independence as he would manage. One can argue, of course, that it was no such thing, that Marcus fell to the politico Ruggiero as he would have fallen to anyone with credentials of a sort who pressed him hard enough, or merely that in his desperation he was prepared to parcel out the Jerome Park reservoir to anybody in the city who was willing to pay for it—Fried, Orlando, Muccini, anybody and everybody. Still, for once, he went forward on his own without Itkin; he recognized his own baser interest and followed it, to the point of having official letters drawn up that would settle the prize on Oakhill. But then, like the eight-year-old who packs up and runs away from home only to stop and hang around the corner luncheonette until his mother comes to get him, Marcus put the unsigned letters in his desk drawer. The moment's urge to rebel had been quickly subdued; it only remained for Itkin to arrive at the corner, acknowledge the daring gesture, and lead his boy home again.

Marcus's letter to Oakhill had not yet been composed when Itkin returned to New York around Armistice Day (he'd been abroad again), but reports of the contract award were already circulating. Oakhill had been unofficially informed of their good fortune by a friendly Water Department employee, and Henry Fried had already begun yelling betrayal. Motto and Corallo had descended on Itkin's office in his absence and made heated representations of double cross to Charles Rappaport. Now Rappaport somewhat agitatedly conveyed their feelings to Itkin, telling him, "You better call Danny and you better call Tony because they're wild."

Itkin called Motto: "I said, 'Danny, what is this problem?' And he says: 'It's no problem, it's a complete double cross. Henry Fried just called me and told me that he found out that Oakhill was getting the contract. Now, what kind of a game are you playing? You are playing with the wrong people if you're going to play this way.'"

Itkin then met Corallo, who, he maintains, told him: "You know, you are not going to get away with something like that. If that's the way the commissioner is going to play, then he's crazy. I am not going to take it."

All that was left was for Itkin to meet Marcus, and this he did at the Municipal Building on November 22, when the Oakhill letter was already stowed in Marcus's desk drawer. They left his office and walked around the block, as Marcus explained that the Republican legal expert Ruggiero had offered five percent on behalf of Oakhill. A businesslike explanation—but it had a violent effect on Itkin. "You got to be crazy! We owe so much money to Danny and Tony, they'll kill us, and you just can't do it! For the difference of percentage points, you just can't do it!" The scene impressed itself on Marcus's memory: "He was really angry and screaming, 'They'll kill us!'"

According to Itkin, Marcus said, "Oh, what am I going to do?"

At "the top of his lungs," Itkin thereupon put it to his partner: "You have to tell them. I'm not going to tell them. You tell them."

We cannot know to what degree Itkin's show of distraction was simulated for the benefit of Marcus, but perhaps his outburst owed less to his fear of the awful vengeance of the Mafia than to the thought that his relationship with Antonio Corallo was being jeopardized by his feckless friend. Itkin had been seeing Corallo or Motto nearly every day during the fall of 1966, and one must assume that they were not exchanging pleasantries; one must assume that new, potentially lucrative projects were being developed. Now Marcus, scarcely knowing what he was about, threatened with the signing of his name to queer everything. Quite enough to make a more stable man than Herbert Itkin yell murder on the streets of New York.

Yet he might have spared himself, for his pupil was anything but intractable. Returning from the walk around the block, Marcus called in engineer Groopman and announced that he had changed his mind. The change, he explained, had something to do with political pressures. Now he was going to award the contract to the engineers' choice, S. T. Grand, after all. That would make him feel easier, he said, because Grand was a large company with a good deal of equipment. He returned to Groopman the letters prepared for Oakhill, which Groopman—who seems to have adjusted calmly to the humors of his politically appointed chief—in turn passed on to his secretary with instructions that they be retyped word for word—except that the firm's name wherever it appeared be changed to S. T. Grand. The secretary followed those instructions precisely, copying even the date, November 18, although the new letter was in fact typed on November 23. She had, in dutiful inadvertence, adjusted history.

So it came about that shortly before Thanksgiving Day, 1966, S. T. Grand, Henry Fried presiding, was awarded the contract to clean the Jerome Park reservoir. The last word on the matter may be left to Herbert Itkin, that minion of the law, who lamented: "The thing that appalled me the most was the hard, ingrained people who have been taking bribes and polluting the city for many years."

SEVEN

The Businessman

*"There is only one thing that you
got to be aware of, and that is
to make sure that whatever you
do, you do it properly."*
HENRY FRIED

D URING the long, lazy course of the reservoir negotiations, which ran from the spring into the fall of 1966,
the president of S. T. Grand met James Marcus only once,
in the company of Vincent Albano, and he never spoke to
Herbert Itkin or, so far as we know, to Daniel Motto. He
explained at his trial that he had relied on his long-time
associate, the late Joseph Pizzo, and his dear friend, the
young Carl D'Angelo, to do what business had to be done
—a service which D'Angelo denies performing. (Fried
had obvious reason in his trial to emphasize the role
played by D'Angelo, but neither Itkin nor Marcus, the
government's main witnesses, was able to confirm, out of
first-hand knowledge, D'Angelo's part in the Fried-Motto
transaction. Itkin now says he considers D'Angelo to have
been merely a messenger.) Motto, who at times regaled
Itkin and Marcus with intimations of the intimacy that he
enjoyed with Henry Fried, may actually have met the contractor only after the reservoir had been cleaned, at
Fried's big horse farm in Germantown, New York, where
he was taken in the summer of 1967 by young Carl. As

Motto told a grand jury, "I know him [Fried] through Carl D'Angelo. I went up to his farm. Carl brang me up to his farm." What transpired between Fried and Motto during their day together, outside of some chitchat about their shared interest in animals ("He told me about his trotters," said Fried, "and I told him about my race horses"), must be left to surmise. It was at about the same time, in the summer of 1967, that Fried first met Itkin and attempted to develop his nodding acquaintance with Marcus.

Whereas Corallo and Motto chose not to avail themselves of the opportunity to testify in their own defense during the 1968 trial, Henry Fried did take the stand. His story, which the jury did not credit, was simple. The emergency contract for the reservoir had been obtained by S. T. Grand in the ordinary course of business, and he knew nothing of any payoff, or what he prefers to call a "finder's fee," until November 25, 1966, after he had received the altered letter from Commissioner Marcus, notifying him of S. T. Grand's selection. As Fried tells it, this welcome news was soured within the hour by a visit from Carl D'Angelo. Appearing in Fried's office unannounced, as he often did, D'Angelo is supposed to have said, "Commissioner, congratulations! [Several of Fried's associates used this form of address, in remembrance of his term as a New York State commissioner of correction under Governor Harriman.] I understand you just got the Jerome Park reservoir, and I want you to know that I helped you get this job." The greeting, alleges Fried, was followed hard by a request for "a five-percent finder's fee." Fried tells us that he protested with vigor and outrage—"I have never paid any finder's fee for any city contract, other than this one, in the history of my business"—and ended by telling the young man to get the hell out of his office.

Two days later, by Fried's account, Joe Pizzo paid him a visit: "He came into my office and he said to me, 'Commish, what the hell are you trying to do, eat up the whole world?'

"I said, 'Joe, I don't know what you're talking about.'

"He said, 'You know this reservoir job. Do you know that was supposed to go to somebody else?'

"I said, 'I don't know anything about that. After all, my engineer was down on two occasions with the City of New York engineers, and so far as I am concerned, we got this job on our merit.' I said this to him.

"Then he said to me, 'Commish, I don't want any trouble with you. You do as your lawyer tells you to.'

"So I said to him, 'Now listen, Joe, you're unreasonable. I don't, again, know what you're talking about. So far as I am concerned, this is an emergency order. I don't have to go through with this job, there is no bond up. I just as soon send my engineer down, tell them we don't want this job.'

"He said, 'Commish, you will pay the finder's fee whether you do this job or not.'

"This was a serious command as far as I was concerned. He also said to me, 'I know what you're doing with my men, or all your men on the outside. You're buying them coffee; they put in over a thousand feet, you're buying them beer. So far as you are concerned, all I want you to do is, again, do as that lawyer tells you to, because if I make up my mind—and I don't want to have any trouble with you,' he said—'Commish, and I slow down your drill runners, slow down your laborers, slow down your engineers, have you any idea what that will cost you?'

"Well, when he made that threat to me, here I was again at his mercy. Knowing of his past, knowing the way he operates, knowing that if he so decided he could put me out of business, here again I started and I tried to talk to him and say to him, with no avail, I said, 'Joe, I can't understand this. Why can't we settle this thing?' And I mentioned fifteen thousand dollars to him.

"He said, 'Do you realize that if I make up my mind and don't cooperate with you, it might cost you one hundred and forty thousand dollars?'

"Well, here I was again at his mercy, knowing his background, knowing his power, knowing his tactics, me personally knowing what he did in Queens about eight, nine years ago, where he extorted some money from a woman who I know very well to the extent of twenty-five thousand dollars. After talking to him, continuing to hate the situation, I couldn't get anywhere with him, and in conclusion he said to me, 'You listen to your lawyer.' "

Whatever our opinions of Fried's claims to an innocence nearly beyond mortal reach, not to speak of the reach of a New York contractor, something like such a conversation probably did take place (the "Commish" lines are too good to be untrue)—when Pizzo made his original approach to S. T. Grand in behalf of Corallo & Co. At that time, the combine was asking for fifteen percent of the contract, an exorbitant figure by going standards, and it is not improbable that Fried balked and bargained or that Pizzo talked tough. They had been doing business together for many years, as Pizzo kept Fried's drill runners and laborers from creating nuisances, and, we may assume, by now they understood one another and were not unduly put off by rude remarks uttered in the heat of haggling. Both knew that the fifteen-percent demand was unrealistic; Fried, offering first $15,000 and subsequently raising his offer to $25,000, was approaching the acceptable five-percent figure. No doubt there was a touch of extortion in Pizzo's method of doing business—but then what could have seemed extraordinary to his associate of so many years about a business deal being touched with extortion?

The jury at Fried's trial in June 1968 found it impossible to accept his claim to truthfulness—"I have been telling the truth all my life. That is as to why I was so successful." He conceded that his testimony to the grand jury the previous December, where he had denied making any payoff on the reservoir contract, was false. For this lapse, he blamed the deceased Pizzo, who, he said, approached him as he was waiting to be called and put him on notice, "Commish, you are going into the grand-jury room and you want to make goddam sure you testify no money was passed or you are apt to find your body in an empty lot." But Pizzo's death four months after Fried's grand-jury appearance did not send the contractor hurrying to the federal prosecutor with the truth. His acknowledgment that he had paid a "finder's fee" was delayed until he had had an opportunity to weigh the strength of the Marcus-Itkin testimony. He also testified that Carl D'Angelo became his enemy at the moment he asked for five percent of the contract: "The moment this thing happened I dumped him. . . . certainly after what he did to me a person would have to be insane to keep him on the payroll." But, in fact, he did not separate the young man from his employ until more than a year later, after the indictment was handed down, and to judge by gifts exchanged, they seem to have enjoyed a most cordial relationship in the meantime.*

Fried's task of satisfying the jury of his innocence was made the more difficult by his outstandingly successful career. At the age of sixty-eight, he had enjoyed many years of prosperity as a leading New York contractor. The dozen corporations he and his four brothers, George, Richard, Hugo, and Oscar, controlled were worth at least $10 million. (Richard went to prison for grand larceny in 1929, and Hugo was put away in 1935 for receiving stolen property.) When Henry Fried said, "I consider myself a fairly good businessman," it was an untypical understatement. Now, a businessman who depends upon government contracts for a significant portion of his income does not become rich by ignoring the reigning politicians. This is axiomatic on all levels of government—we need only recall the care taken by the House of Morgan in its great years to let important Democrats as well as important Republicans in on its stock bonanzas. In Fried's case, sound business practice required that he be on as friendly terms with Carmine De Sapio during De Sapio's years as Demo-

---

* Fried's testimony was interesting for its use of specific detail. In reporting on a meeting, for example, he would rarely fail to mention that he ordered a cup of coffee or a Coke, in the way that manufacturers of shoddy goods will rely on a decorative touch to distract the consumer's eye. This technique got him into trouble now and then. He recalled that in reply to Carl D'Angelo's demand for five percent, he said, "Now, Carl, I don't like this, and you know darn well that I was in the hospital in February for a coronary deficiency, and I don't want to excite myself with you." This plea lost some of its impact when it was pointed out that the conversation took place about three months *before* Fried went into the hospital. The witness apologized: "I just was a little ahead of my story." It was not the only instance of Fried's tendency to adjust dates.

cratic boss and afterwards as he was with the Republican boss Vincent Albano. Henry Fried, like Daniel Motto, understood that there are no politics in politics. Despite his position as a director of the National Democratic Club, which named him Man of the Year in New York City in 1966,* he made generous contributions to both political parties, bought tickets for the testimonial dinners of both parties, and invited dignitaries of both parties to the gala opening of his horse farm in Germantown in August 1967. (Motto was miffed at not being asked to the party despite the affection for horses which he shared with the host— but his status as a labor leader did not entitle him to recognition at an affair that could boast the presence of George Meany.) At Fried's party, one might have encountered that "universal camaraderie, with not a touch of friendship about it," which Lord Bryce found at a Tweed-run Democratic convention in Rochester.

The attraction between businessmen and politicians is not confined to these shores or to this century. It is among the oldest of civic relationships; it is free of ideology; and its nature is more clear than other forms of magnetism. The businessman, as Lincoln Steffens taught us, "is the chief source of corruption." The money that he pays out may be in the form of a contribution, a gift (the books of S. T. Grand indicated that the corporation distributed $53,000 as "gifts" at Christmastime, 1967), a bribe. The favor received may range from a warm introduction to a cool deal. The grossest arrangements, needless to say, are impermissible, but participants in civic affairs have con-

* In 1965 Fried was Man of the Year for the Friendly Sons of Saint Joseph, in Westchester County. In 1964 he was Man of the Year for the Veterans of Foreign Wars.

cluded that overzealous policing results in a loss of efficiency; a little "honest graft," it has long been appreciated, is in fact a lubricant for progress.

Still, lubricants may, if used without due care, leave a mess, and the Marcus case was not the first time that Henry Fried found himself implicated in the compromising of a public official. In 1952 a New York City councilman named Hugh Quinn introduced a bill to permit the use in the city of fly ash (a residue of burning pulverized coal in suspension) as an additive in reinforced concrete and a partial substitute for cement. The bill was signed into law in May 1953, and a few days later Quinn was hired, part-time, at a salary above what he was earning as a councilman, by Triboro Carting, one of Fried's companies. (The city's carting industry has never enjoyed much of a reputation. In the uncontradicted description of an assistant corporation counsel, it has traditionally been "marked by price-fixing, chiseling, and racketeering." He could not forbear from adding that it "has been in bad odor for years.") The event assumes a dubious cast when we note that Triboro had a $400,000-a-year contract with Consolidated Edison for removing fly ash from its plants. In opening new markets for the waste substance, Quinn's bill constituted a windfall for Fried's company.

This remarkable series of events did not come to the public attention until October 1956, when Quinn, still a councilman as well as a Fried employee, introduced another bill of special interest to Triboro Carting. This one would have specifically exempted cartmen hauling ashes and debris from building-demolition jobs from the regular city provisions controlling private garbage collection. Nor did this exhaust the councilman's solicitude for the Fried operations. He had over the years appeared before the city's Board of Standards and Appeals as representative for two of his private employer's realty firms—in acknowledgment of which he was given an interest in one of the firms. An investigation into these events by the City Council resulted in two resignations: Quinn abruptly gave up the council seat which he had held since 1938, and Fried reluctantly resigned his honorary post with the State Correction Commission to which he had been appointed in 1955 on the recommendation of Carmine De Sapio, in recognition of his abiding concern for the rehabilitation of former convicts and the Democratic Party.

As we come upon such instances of easy dealing, the question obtrudes itself: can a businessman grow rich in serving any large city without giving way to the temptation to tempt others? Especially when so many of the others have come to expect, to require tempting. Fried was prone to ambiguous relationships, excessively prone perhaps—but he was operating in an area where such relationships are bred by the climate; the germs feed in the soil and are carried on the winds. Not all residents are sticken, but it seems inordinately difficult for one to prosper in such an environment and still get through life with honor reasonably intact. Even without the Marcus involvement, Henry Fried was on his way toward meriting the tribute which Gibbon laid on the Roman general who retired his military command "with an ample fortune and a suspicious integrity."

The Jerome Park deal had now been made, the contract let. On December 5, 1966, S. T. Grand's bulldozers began their attack on the long-accumulated sludge of the drained reservoir; and, in Marcus's words, "We were look-ing to get paid." He and Itkin had assumed that the entire payoff, which they figured at about $50,000, would be made directly on the letting of the contract, but they reck-oned without the experienced businessman's distaste for premature payments. Money, which breeds more money simply by existing, is too valuable to be let go of until the last moment, and Fried was only observing this basic rule when, as he says, he told Carl D'Angelo that he would pay "this finder's fee" after he received his own payment from the city.

The payoff, serious matter though it was, exudes a spirit of farce, like one of those spy spoofs where it is difficult to sort out ally from enemy, with everyone busy chasing and ducking everyone else. For many weeks, Motto had been badgering Marcus and Itkin, with near-daily calls and meetings, to award the contract; now, the contract having been awarded, it was their turn to bother him. Suddenly Motto was hard to reach. Marcus's calls were not reward-ing: "Sometimes there was no answer, sometimes he was out; he would be back, he would return the call, but he didn't return the call." For two weeks Itkin, under pres-sure from Corallo to collect the bribe, also tried to contact Motto, with no greater success. At last Motto, who was in turn being stalled by Fried, agreed to meet with Itkin, Marcus, and Corallo in Itkin's office. Before this meeting, which took place around December 10, Corallo directed Itkin to "put it on strong" to Motto. "I don't see why we don't have our money," said the veteran racketeer, but for some reason he was reluctant to put it on strong to Motto himself, in the way that Plumeri had to Zulferino and Berger. Itkin testified that Corallo explained to him that he didn't want to apply pressure directly on Motto because "if I start with him, it's going to be a fuss, and if I ever have to make a fuss, I'll make it when there is a real reason." Such are the restraints imposed on great powers in dealing with their lesser allies. For now, Corallo assured Itkin: "I'm behind you."

When Marcus got to the office on December 10, Itkin greeted him privately. He conveyed Corallo's expression of support and, like a Saturday afternoon coach, urged, "Go in and raise hell with Danny."

Marcus girded himself and did as he was bid: "Danny, you screamed and you yelled and you wanted your thing. Now I've done it. I've completed the contract. Where is the money?"

Motto, the middleman in the payoff, did what he could to pacify his friends. Fried, he explained, was experienced in these matters and now contended that he could not be expected to pay the entire five percent at the outset because no one yet knew what the job would cost. However, he had agreed to make a down payment of a quarter of the bribe, based on the estimate of a million-dollar contract. That was acceptable to Corallo, and Motto assured everyone that he could get the amount "in a minute's notice," whereupon the meeting broke up, more or less amicably.

It would be considerably more than a minute, indeed more than a month, before the initial payment, time enough for Marcus to receive a discouraging bit of clarification. On a stroll with Itkin around the Municipal Building one day in December (Itkin thinks it may even have been after the first payment), Marcus learned that he had "misconstrued" the three-two division of the payoff approved by Corallo. It was to be one percent apiece for Corallo and Motto, leaving three percent, which Marcus had believed was all his, to be shared with Itkin. When the commissioner protested that it was "a hell of a time to tell me," Itkin consoled him with the reminder that "we have a lot of other things that we are working on." Itkin had no cause to share Marcus's disappointment: indeed, it is very likely that he intentionally held up clarifying the three-two deal until the last moment, or beyond. The arrangement ordered by Corallo was plainly acceptable to him—for who would not prefer to share three percent with friend Marcus rather than two percent with Motto-Corallo? Whatever fight there may have been in James Marcus, it seems to have been drained out of him like the water from the reservoir. "There isn't very much that we can do," he sighed. "The contract has already been let."

In the meantime, Motto, without personal access to Henry Fried, was applying what pressure he could through go-betweens. According to Fried, after he told D'Angelo that the "finder's fee" would not be paid until he got his money from the city, Joe Pizzo reappeared. As they were sipping coffee in a drugstore near Rockefeller Center, Pizzo opened the subject: "Commish, what are you giving me, some trouble?"

"I don't know what you're talking about."

"I understand you talked to Carl D'Angelo."

"Yes."

"And you told him you're going to pay Carl when you get the money. Now, cut out these shenanigans. You pay us when you bill the city."

It was at this meeting that Fried claims he raised his offer to Pizzo, from $15,000 to $25,000, to settle the whole matter—but such a double cross after the letting of the contract could only have created trouble all around, including for Pizzo's senior associate Corallo, who had in mind a continuing relationship with Marcus-Itkin. So Pizzo replied, "Will you stop bothering me. I've got a commitment here. You do as your lawyer tells you." We may believe Fried when he says that "every time I made a payment I had hatred in my heart." That is a normal reaction to having to make payments.

In the nature of things, the hour when spoils must be collected and shared, like the hour when a ship approaches land, is a perilous one. Alliances may then be shaken by the waves of temptation or grounded on the shoals of suspicion or dashed upon the rocks of revenge. As the evolution of democratic society has carried us past the era when grateful entrepreneurs could make their donatives directly to deserving officials, new opportunities have opened to middlemen. In the present case, as 1966 turned into 1967, the businessman Fried had but briefly encountered the official Marcus and had yet to lay eyes on Itkin or, he says, Motto. He made all his payments, he swears, to Carl D'Angelo—which, swears D'Angelo, he did not. To whomever the cash was paid, it reached Itkin via Motto; no receipts were kept; and the space between briber and bribed invited thoughts of murky doings in the pitch of night.

The total contract, as it turned out, would amount to $841,316—five percent of which, owed by Fried to the combine, came to something over $42,000. The Marcus-Itkin share was to be roughly $28,000, down somewhat from the $75,000 that had danced in their heads the previous spring. And even this reduced sum would never find its way to them in full.

Fried's first payment was made in January 1967. Itkin was off on European journeys for much of that month, and so Charles Rappaport was left with instructions to keep after Motto. Corallo told the young man, "Charlie, you stay on this guy and get the money and say that I am angry and that I need it. I am spending money on trips and I want the money."

On his return to New York, Itkin was informed by Rappaport that the money had been handed over—"but you're going to be mighty disappointed." Motto had received an installment of $10,000 from Fried, which should have meant a cut of $6,000 for Marcus-Itkin. But Motto had decided to keep $5,250 of their share as repayment of the $5,000 loan he had made to the pair three months before, "plus the accrued vig." That left just $750 for Marcus-Itkin. When Rappaport complained, Motto gave him another thousand dollars. This money, like all subsequent payments, was put in a Marcus-Itkin joint account, in the nominal charge of Rappaport, and was used to pay off interest on loans as well as to take care of Charlie Rappaport's wages and keep Itkin in pocket money. Marcus seems to have had only a distant notion of how the money was being managed, though Itkin allowed him to understand that it was for their mutual benefit.

There were no further payments in January or in February, presumably because Fried had not yet sent his first bill to the city. Corallo kept pushing Itkin to push Motto during these weeks, claiming that he had yet to get his share of the first $10,000 payment: "I don't understand this deal. So far I've gotten nothing, and I don't want to have it out with Danny. Push him. But you pick up the money the next time and give it to me right away."

The next time came in the middle of March. Itkin got a call from Motto to meet him at his accustomed parking space on Forty-sixth Street: "I have something for you." Itkin hastened over but arrived after Mrs. Motto had already finished work and joined her husband. Reluctant to do his business while his wife watched, Motto said, "Come on, take a walk with me." They walked down the street to the Roosevelt Hotel and went into the men's room. There Motto handed Itkin $3,000 (Fried evidently having delivered an installment of $5,000). Itkin also took $1,000 for Corallo, who, alerted, was waiting back at his office.

When pressed for faster collection, Motto would shunt responsibility to Carl D'Angelo. "Danny, where is it?" Itkin would urge. "It should be due by now." And Motto would reply: "Any day. I called Carl." Or "Carl told me Henry is about to do it." Or "Carl forgot and he had something else to do and couldn't pick it up."

During such a conversation one day in April, Motto announced that he had "a definite appointment" with Henry Fried and would come afterwards to Itkin's office to meet with Itkin and Corallo. But, when he arrived, it was only to report that he had been granted the reception often accorded to importuning creditors: Fried had sent word that he was too busy to see him.

Corallo, not accustomed to that kind of highhandedness from businessmen in his debt, showed fine restraint. "Danny," he said, "do me a favor. Call him now, will you, and tell him you're coming over. Just do me a favor."

Motto sulked: "I was just there."

"I'm asking you to please do me a favor and call him."

Motto performed the favor. He called, apparently reached Carl D'Angelo, and said, "I'm coming up for that thing. See that you get it." He hung up. "Okay, I'm going up there, I'm going to see that I get it. I'll see you fellows later."

But Corallo, out of mistrust or just annoyance, had another thought. "No," he said, and turned to Itkin. "You go along with him, Herbie. I'm going to wait here."

Itkin accompanied Motto to Rockefeller Center, the vicinity of Fried's headquarters; Motto made a call, again presumably to D'Angelo, and announced, "I'm here and I'm coming up for the package." Up he went; down he came; and in a coffee shop at Sixth Avenue and Fiftieth Street, he passed Itkin, literally under the table, $3,000, plus $1,000 for Corallo. The remarkably prompt service suggests that Motto had had the cash with him but wanted to hold on to it for a while longer at least. It also indicates that Corallo knew with whom he was dealing.

At the fourth payment, made about a week later, Corallo evidently decided to test Motto. He waited at Itkin's Madison Avenue office, while Itkin joined Motto at Rockefeller Center and then, in the car driving back to the office, received an installment of $3,000. Itkin said, "Don't give me Tony's money. I'm not going to see him." Back at the office, he informed Corallo that Danny was holding his $1,000. If Corallo ever received that $1,000, he received it late—yet, for some reason, he was still unwilling to apply directly to Motto. We do not know enough about their past relationship to interpret such an unexpected inhibition. It is also possible, of course, that Corallo had in fact been getting his share along with the others but was putting on something of an act as preparation for taking practically all of the fifth payment for himself.

On the occasion of this payment, in the middle of May, Corallo directed that Motto bring the whole $5,000 to Itkin's office. There, with Itkin present and Marcus waiting in another room, Corallo made his move: "Put the money down on the table and let me explain something. I haven't been getting my share. I've laid out a lot of money in other things. I want it off the top now." Then, amid some bickering, he coolly pocketed most of the cash, leaving just $500 for Marcus-Itkin.

"This is insane!" protested Itkin, and he warned that the commissioner, who was pacing without, would be displeased.

Not noticeably affrighted, Corallo said, "Well, go tell him, and tell him that we just had a lot of expenses."

Marcus, as foreseen, was displeased. He roused himself to a boyish threat: "That's the last deal I'm going through with these fellows."

Itkin bore this fierce response back to these fellows: "Well, I did just what you said, but I don't think he's ever going to play ball with us, and I think you're silly, because if we're going to go ahead in the other deals, then I think it's best that you take care of him now." (Itkin was a remarkably well-adjusted middleman. Whether talking with Corallo, with Marcus, or with his F.B.I. contact, he fell easily into the first-person plural. When he wasn't near the partner he loved, he loved the partner he was near.)

Earlier, Marcus had complained to Corallo that Motto had been charging "vig" on the money that he and Itkin had borrowed. Corallo had seemed surprised, and now he said, "Danny, all right, you and I will each give him a hundred dollars more."

In what may stand as the most ignominious scene of this history, Motto took Marcus into the men's room, handed him two $100 bills, and said, "Here, this is for you." He then turned and walked out. Back in the office, Motto reported, "All right I gave it to him. He's happy." *

* This transaction occurred close to May 11, the day of the reopening of the reservoir. Motto approached Itkin to ask whether the commissioner might arrange to have a photograph snapped of Henry Fried and John Lindsay smiling at one another on that occasion. Whether this was a spontaneous gesture on the part of Motto, seeking to bolster his tenuous connection with Fried, or merely the relaying of Fried's own desire, as transmitted through D'Angelo, we do not know. Marcus, showing a decent regard for the public face of the friend who had raised him so high, said that he didn't think he could arrange the performance, and so, on the big day, Lindsay and Marcus took a helicopter to the Bronx and had themselves photographed opening the sluice gates without Henry Fried's help.

EIGHT

The $10,000 Misunderstanding

*"With the monstrosity of my
business, the books never
did interest me."*
HENRY FRIED

THE $200 tip in the men's room was the last payment
that James Marcus would dredge from the Jerome
Park reservoir, once the reservoir of his dreams. About
thirty-five years ago, a reporter of corruption in New York
City laid down the rule that the use of a middleman in the
passing of bribes "requires only two things, a principal
who will submit to the extortion and an attorney who will
retain no more than his agreed share after he has received
the cash." The reservoir deal had a surplus of middlemen,
not all lawyers; and at least one of them seems to have
decided that he deserved or could get away with more
than his share. "Everybody screws everybody in these
cases," shrugs Itkin.

By Itkin's calculations, the combine had gotten only
$30,000, in five payments, since the letting of the contract,
and so he continued calling the evasive Motto. At length,
early in June 1967, Motto asked Itkin to come up to his
office in Long Island City. There he told him: "You know,
you're screaming for another payment. Henry Fried just
showed me a little book which shows seven payoffs. Now,

what are you talking about? There is very little money left for us."

Pointing out that Itkin was given to "running back and forth all over the world," Motto graciously suggested that Rappaport had picked up an extra payment or two and neglected to mention it. "You go back and talk to Charlie, and you tell him—but there is nothing really left for us. It's only a few thousand dollars."

When, in the presence of Tony Ducks, Itkin put Motto's thought to Rappaport—"Charlie, Danny says you picked up three payments . . ."—the young lawyer denied it emphatically, not to say frantically: "I didn't! I swear to you I didn't!"

Corallo told him not to get excited, and ordered a meeting once again, "to put it on Danny." He promised support for Itkin and Rappaport: "Don't give in. I'll be there, and we'll have other people there. But something has to be done about this."

The meeting, to which Corallo brought an unidentified man whose presence presumably was meant to mean something to Motto, took place soon afterwards at a First Avenue luncheonette. After Itkin reviewed the five payments picked up by himself and Rappaport, Motto won the day with the following argument: "You must be confused. I'm telling you, I saw it in Henry's book, and the man wouldn't make a mistake. He has the dates. Are you keeping records?" Itkin and Rappaport conceded that they kept no records of such transactions, whereupon Motto, who may or may not actually have met Fried at this juncture, capped his proof: "Henry Fried must be right. He has it down in a book."

Corallo broke off the discussion: "I heard enough. I'm sick. I don't want to hear another word." On being told that there was about $2,500 outstanding, he ruled that $1,000 must go to Joe Pizzo ("I'm embarrassed about all the work he did, he's gotten nothing yet") and the remainder would go to Marcus. A few days later Motto indicated to Itkin that he had been up to see Fried, and all that was coming to the combine, for unexplained reasons, was $1,600.

Henry Fried, in his testimony, concurred in Motto's story to an extent—he insisted that he had paid out $40,000. But he denied possessing a little black book, or having had any personal contact with Motto other than their pleasant day at his horse farm. He said that he had put his firm's controller on notice that every billing to the city on the reservoir job entailed a five-percent payment, in cash, to Carl D'Angelo. Sometimes, Fried said, he personally passed on the money; sometimes the controller did it. Once, he said, D'Angelo complained that payments were short by $5,000, but the controller set him right. Otherwise, Fried was hazy on such details as whether the transaction was noted in his firm's books: "I am not a bookkeeper . . . in my operation of twenty million dollars a year, I never bothered with the books." Nor was he certain on which of his several corporations the money was drawn: "All these corporations, so far as I was concerned, were a family affair." According to the U.S. Attorney's office, miscellaneous checks payable to cash and to Fried and his brothers from their family affair in 1966 and 1967 totaled $267,000.

The great mystery of the missing $10,000 remains unresolved. Did Fried in fact pay only $30,000 by oversight?

("With the monstrosity of my business, the books never did interest me.") Did he in fact keep a little black book—and tamper with the entries? Might his controller have pocketed the loose bills? Or might D'Angelo have kept a couple of payments for himself . . . or might he have shared them with his friend and client Motto . . . or might Motto have kept them . . . or shared them with Corallo or even Itkin? (Was Corallo's show of exasperation—"This is insane! . . . You are all a bunch of screwballs!"—only an act?) Did Motto actually pass on the money to Rappaport and Itkin, and did one or the two together keep some of it, despite perspiring avowals of innocence? Such were the conditions of this conspiracy and the quality of the conspirators that none of the foregoing possibilities, by itself or in combination, can be scratched out. Still, if one must choose, one is bound to agree with Itkin that the likeliest suspect was Daniel Motto. In the position of middleman between middlemen, he was strategically located for holding the cash and imputing blame on others; his whole attitude since the signing of the contract had been less than fraternal.

What is striking about this entire incident and its anticlimatic resolution is the passivity with which the losers took their loss. Not a threatening word seems to have escaped anyone's lips. By all the myths of the Mafia, Antonio Corallo should with a glance have been able to bring Motto and the others to heel; but instead he fumed a bit, sighed a bit, and let it go at that. We need not conclude from this example of forebearance that the Mafia has been defamed these many years and is unconnected with weighted bodies in the nation's waterways. Corallo was well on the far side of the generation gap; his blood had

had time to cool; and though a certain reputation might still be of use for dealings of a certain sort, sheer muscle was not as important in his present career as once it may have been. An honest living, to be sure, was out of the question for him—but then that is beyond quite a number of reputable businessmen. Given the boundaries within which he was accustomed to operate, he could still behave in a civilized manner. Age and prosperity seem to have brought a similar self-image to the late Joe Pizzo. Moreover, in the Marcus-Itkin situation, there was always the risk that a show of violence might frighten away the goose that still had within it a golden egg or two.

Whereas Motto seems to have determined to grab what he could from the reservoir deal, even at the expense of leaving a residue of bad feeling, Corallo was looking to the future. (His reluctance to pressure Motto may have been part of an understanding between the two that allotted the missing thousands to Motto as a finder's fee for bringing Marcus-Itkin within the precincts of Corallo.) Through the summer and into the fall of 1967, Corallo was a frequent visitor to Itkin's office and to his apartment on East Fifteenth Street, where they were occasionally joined by Marcus. There had been small profit so far for an operator of Corallo's reputation and presumed expectations. His good offices in the reservoir deal may be viewed as an investment and his subsequent meetings with Itkin and Marcus as a means of making that investment show a profit. For example, among the numerous city officials to whom Marcus introduced Herbert Itkin was the Housing Administrator—"because Mr. Corallo was interested in getting some housing projects."

Henry Fried, too, wished to improve on his still-distant acquaintance with Commissioner Marcus, whom he had encountered but once since the introduction by Vincent Albano, and then only in passing and in the presence of others, while dropping by for a look at the reservoir. Fried, as we have seen, was not backward about building up cordial relations with politicians and officeholders and, we may infer, owed some portion of his success to his outgoing spirit. In calling Marcus repeatedly during the early months of 1967, with invitations for lunch or a drink, he was only seeking to carry on business as usual. But Marcus, showing unwonted discretion, ducked him. The reservoir was still being cleaned; the city was still being billed; payoffs were still being made. It was premature to begin a friendship with Henry Fried.

Moreover, it may be that Marcus still did not feel comfortable in the conspirator's cloak; as he concedes, he didn't know the rules, and his easygoing temperament served him ill in negotiations with Mottoesque types. Yet, he wanted what Fried had to offer, and in July, when work on the reservoir had been completed and the contractor renewed his invitations for a drink, Marcus accepted—but asked Itkin to come along. Itkin agreed—and with his instinct for such matters, he suggested that after introductions had been made and preliminary chitchat gotten over, Marcus should excuse himself to make a phone call—"and I will see what he really wants."

Fried's opening gambit at the July 1967 meeting with Marcus and Itkin in the lounge of the Hotel Commodore, though it skirted the main object in his mind, was not a model of subtlety. But then uncommon subtlety is no particular asset to a contractor, and his approach suggests that Fried, like any youth with a line for the Saturday night dance, had developed a formula for getting better acquainted with persons who struck his fancy. He quickly mastered his annoyance at finding Marcus accompanied by a third party, who was introduced by the commissioner as his "confidant, adviser, and friend," and launched into a description of his breeding farm in Germantown, then being readied for its grand opening in August. He spoke of its great size, its indoor track and steam-heated stalls, its electronic controls: "It is an amazing thing." (In a fit of social mobility, Henry Fried had leaped into the landed gentry, raising horses on his estate just like the Vanderbilts. But he had not yet learned how to enjoy such a possession without bragging about it to the likes of Itkin and Marcus. A generation or two of seasoning is required for the art of understatement. Still, in Itkin he found a suitable audience. Fried recalls an engaging bit of Itkin dialogue from their first meeting: "He said to me, 'Fried, you and I have something in common. If you got time, I would like to take you with me on a plane and go to London. I got some horses out there.' He said, 'You know, in London the horses run just the reverse of our horses here.'") Fried also talked about his boat: "Any time you want to go, anybody you want to bring, just let me know, and the boat is at your disposal. . . . Just call me and I will have a captain and a crew prepared for you." He suggested a weekend sail. He suggested that "it might be fun if we all got together and went out to the race track in it."

Marcus put him off politely by explaining that he and his family spent their summer weekends in Maine. (Did he let drop a reminder, as he swept past Fried's boats and horses, that his wife was the daughter and he the son-in-law of a Lodge?) But Itkin, ever at the ready, responded in kind. He urged Fried to invest, through him, in the Dominican Republic: "There is an area where you can really develop property if you have the money to go in big enough and buy beach front." He pulled out a map and explained that with Cuba lost to the West, the Dominican Republic was in for a tourist boom. It was a hard sell: "I would like to have you in here for about twenty-five thousand dollars." Far too experienced in deals to send his money south with Herbert Itkin, Fried said he'd look into it. They were like a pair of old wrestlers, circling one another, watchful for an opening.

In this Aesopian manner was the stage set for serious discussion. Marcus got up from the table, mumbled something about having to make a few phone calls, and told Fried, "Anything you have to say you can say to Mr. Itkin." The two sharpers were left alone.

The gist of Fried's message, in Itkin's summary version of their fifteen-minute chat, was as follows: "I'm a lot older than you are and you are handling your deals with the city terribly, and if you will listen to me you won't get hurt, and you are handling it very badly. First of all, there is no reason to share with these other guys. What have you got to do with these type of people? Do you know that I can handle the biggest payoffs in the city?" Fried's whole effort at this meeting was to break through the Pizzo-Corallo-Motto barrier between himself and the commissioner. What did three nice Jewish boys have to do with this type of people? Had Fried been anything of a reader, he could have summed up his attitude toward their accomplices with a quote from Flaubert: "There are some men whose only function in life is to act as intermediaries; one crosses them as if they were bridges and leaves them behind." Itkin says that when he brought up the subject of the reservoir payoff, Fried insisted that he had paid the full $40,000, and would pay the remaining $1,600 to Danny Motto within the week. (At the opening of the horse farm, according to Itkin, Fried assured him that the $1,600 had finally been paid. Paid or not, the money never reached Marcus-Itkin.)

Marcus returned from his phone calls, and the sparring match broke up. As they watched Fried leave the hotel, Marcus asked Itkin what he had wanted, and Itkin replied, "He wants to do business with us. . . . He wants to go around Tony and Danny."

Fried offers a different version of this meeting. He denies putting forward any propositions and contends that the main topic was the Dominican Republic, into which he refused to be inveigled by Itkin. The meeting, he said, had been set up by his friendly competitor, Edward Orlando, and he had gone along only as a favor to Orlando, who, with his father, was present throughout. In detailing this version, Fried fell into a number of contradictions, which, taken together with an inherent implausibility, relieve us of the task of weighing it against the Marcus-Itkin story. No doubt Itkin was, as usual, seeking an "investment" from Fried in the Dominican Republic, and it is understandable that Fried, his mind on deals of his own, should have interpreted Itkin's solicitations as part of a *quid pro quo*. But Fried, we may be certain, did not take the time and trouble to go to the Commodore merely to oblige the Orlandos.*

* Under questioning by his attorney at his trial, Fried gave this unsolicited recollection from his meeting with Itkin: "Then out of a clear

The place that the Orlandos held in Fried's aspiring relationship with Marcus-Itkin became clearer at a second meeting at the Commodore in August, this one attended by Fried, Itkin, and Edward Orlando. Several matters were discussed. There was old business: Fried again promised to pay the $1,600 soon; Itkin again turned on his Dominican Republic spiel, and Fried still demurred despite eager Orlando's agreement to put in $5,000: "I'd be willing to go in for five if you go in for five." And there was new business: Fried and Orlando were planning to engage in a "joint venture" to enhance their ability to serve the City of New York.

This arrangement did not entirely please Itkin or Marcus. Itkin was content to keep up his relationship with Orlando, who had given him several thousand dollars "to do something" in the Dominican Republic; but Fried's penchant for holding back on payoff money was still a sore point. Itkin says that he told Fried outright, "You have left a bad taste in everybody's mouth about cutting the amount of money. . . . You know the people I'm with, and they are very upset about being short-cut." The reference was to Antonio Corallo. The distaste that the contractor felt for the racketeer—"Cut out those fellows," Fried advised Itkin—was amply reciprocated. The influential millionaire Fried being beyond Corallo's control,

---

blue sky he said to me, 'What did you pay on that Jerome reservoir?' He sort of caught me short, and I said, 'Forty thousand dollars.' He said, 'I got to get rid of those hoods!' and he got up and he was very mad." The testimony rings true—both as to Fried's wish to make the point that he had paid the full sum and as to Itkin's reaction. Nonetheless, it is a remarkable admission if we credit Fried's story that Edward Orlando was present during this conversation. It becomes less remarkable if we accept Itkin's version of their first meeting as clearing the ground for a new deal.

Corallo was promoting two other contracting firms which he had reason to believe would pay promptly for favorable treatment by the city. Corallo warned Itkin against the new silent partnership of Fried and Orlando: "I think you ought to stay away from both those guys."

Itkin assured his co-plotter that Orlando, not Fried, would be held responsible for all payoffs. But whatever Itkin's reservations about Fried and his worries about irritating Corallo, the Fried-Orlando arrangement made sense. Orlando, whose contracting concern was much smaller than S. T. Grand, had already made his peace with Marcus-Itkin, in the form of payoffs on emergency contracts. Now word was going around that the city contemplated doing extensive work on the Central Park reservoir. The job was estimated at $1.5 million, surpassing even Jerome Park. So big an undertaking was beyond the competence of Orlando, and Fried did not wish to appear too forward in reaching for it on his own at this time. As Itkin quotes him, "I just finished the Jerome Park job, and it wouldn't be politic for me to get the next reservoir. . . . If I got both big contracts, all hell would break loose." Orlando was to make application to the Water Department to do the Central Park reservoir job, counting on his silent partner to supply equipment, direction, and payoffs as needed. Fried boasted that he could lay hands on $250,-000 in green on twenty-four hours' notice: "Do you think Orlando can do that?" Itkin reminded him that a measly $1,600 was still unpaid, after many weeks: "I just hope that the same thing that happened on Jerome Park doesn't happen on Central Park." As a pledge of his earnest, Fried handed over $1,500 in cash, which Orlando owed for favoritism in the award of an emergency contract. ("We're

like the pebble on the beach compared to Fried," mur-
mured Orlando when charges were brought against him in
January 1968, just a few weeks after he had been Henry
Fried's guest at a dinner for the sheriff of Westchester
County, along with Carmine De Sapio and then Chief In-
spector of the New York City Police Department Sanford
D. Garelik. "I couldn't understand why he was so fond of
me.")

The Central Park reservoir was not destined to be
cleaned by either Orlando or S. T. Grand. The city comp-
troller, whose approval was required, balked at Marcus's
proposal that a $1.5 million contract be let on an emer-
gency basis. It was even suggested that the method of
handling the Jerome Park reservoir might not have been
altogether sound, and Marcus, desperate though he was
for cash, had no wish to stir up sludgy waters. In the Itkin-
Fried meetings of summer 1967, however, Fried raised the
subject of still another set of deals already in the works, an
ambitious project which would for a few months hold
pride of place in the Marcus-Itkin portfolio. It had to do
with the Consolidated Edison Company.

NINE

The Utility

*"Well, apparently there are some
things I didn't have knowledge of. . . ."*
CHARLES F. LUCE, *chairman of the board
of trustees and chief executive officer
of the Consolidated Edison Company
of New York*

THE meager sums paid into the Marcus-Itkin account during 1967 from the Henry Fried bribe and gratuities for other emergency contracts could not begin to repair James Marcus's financial condition. The prospect that he might be fiscally fresh baptized by the waters of the Jerome Park reservoir having proved illusory, he lapsed into despair. Itkin described his state at the time: "He has gotten himself so trapped and so boxed in on the stock that I don't think he knows which end is up any more." Troubled lest his friend's despondency bring a premature end to their partnership, Itkin kept urging him to bestir himself and raise some money, possibly by selling or mortgaging his summer house in Beach Haven, New Jersey. But for once Marcus demurred: "I can't get rid of the Beach Haven house. It is the only thing that keeps me alive now. I run away from everything that is happening in the city, and I walk on the beach there and I feel better."

The demand for cash to meet vigorish payments was unremitting, and it fell to Itkin to find ways to keep Marcus afloat and support himself at the same time. His main recourse was to loans on which the pair was charged between two percent and five percent a week, a hearty advance over the limits sanctioned by the state's usury laws. At one point, according to Marcus, who had a dreamily distant sense of the constant round of loans and repayments being negotiated in his behalf, the vigorish was running at $1,200 a week: "Some of the creditors liked to be paid every Tuesday at a certain hour, and if they weren't—well, it was just best we paid them."

Itkin's energies were divided between assuring loan sharks that they would get their money from the enormous profits soon to be realized on spectacular deals, and trying to rouse Marcus out of his gloom and lethargy with warnings of the loan sharks' revenge. He told Michael Bonfondeo, who had loaned Marcus $20,000 on his introduction, of a nonexistent $1.5 million contract, from which five percent was due to the commissioner: "I wanted him to be comforted by the chance that he would get his money back and not have him reckless." Meanwhile, he told the commissioner that he was further behind on his payments to Bonfondeo than in fact he was, as a way of shaking him up. He warned Marcus that Bonfondeo was capable of calling on him at home and smacking him around in front of his wife: "Jim, you are behind to Bonfondeo. Jim, you promised to pay out of your salary. You borrowed the money, and Michael is the type of fellow that will come up to your house if necessary. Now, for gosh sakes, if you are going to borrow, pay it back. Go borrow from your family, mortgage your house, but get rid of the Shylock." As Joseph Valachi, the famous Mafia informer and sometime usurer has observed, "The idea is not to bust a guy's head. Anybody can do that. The idea is to keep the money moving all the time." Grasping this

127

principle, Itkin managed to pacify Bonfondeo and take off some of the pressure by steering him to another needy friend, who took a loan of $40,000 and, according to Itkin, paid back about $140,000 in the course of a year. For this, Marcus-Itkin received as commission from Bonfondeo a three-percent credit against their debt.

Despite the air of languor that disturbed Itkin, Marcus's dreams had not been entirely extinguished. They flickered still within his slough of despond, awaiting only another big chance, like Xtra, like Jerome Park, to breathe them into fresh life, desperation serving as a powerful bellows. That chance came, the last big one; and it came in the form of an awesome enterprise, the Consolidated Edison Company of New York, purveyor of gas and electricity to the residents of New York City and Westchester County.

The attraction of Con Edison to the small but expanding group of operators privy to the knowledge that the favors of the Commissioner of Water Supply, Gas and Electricity were up for sale was simple in the extreme. The supply of electricity to New Yorkers required the utility to spend some $40 million a year on street construction and repair. Most of this work required approval from Marcus's department. A Con Edison executive puts the relationship plainly: "We can't dig a hole in the street without getting a permit from the Department of Water Supply." Why, mused Antonio Corallo and others, could these two facts not be parlayed into a winning ticket for persons who had invested in the good will of the commissioner?

Of special fascination to the cabal in the spring of 1967 was a huge hydropower complex that Con Edison proposed to build on the Hudson River, at Storm King Mountain near Cornwall, New York. Designed to serve as a power-storing project which could help meet the city's peak electricity needs, the proposal had been under furious attack from conservationists since 1963—but the beauties of the Hudson's highlands and the well-being of the Hudson's fish were far from the thoughts of Itkin's collaborators. What did move them were the beauties of the estimate for the project—around $200 million—and the involvement of the New York City Water Department, owing to the existence at Storm King of an aqueduct that carried down forty percent of the city's water from upstate reservoirs and might conceivably be damaged by the drilling required for the power plant. According to Itkin, in April 1967 Carl D'Angelo, son of Armand, told him, "Herbie, my father gave a letter to Con Edison just before he left office, and it is for what they want. I know what the deal is, and I can get you thirty-five thousand dollars right away in cash if you get Marcus to push the Storm King Mountain thing through, like my father did." Itkin replied cordially that he understood the favor to be worth on the order of a quarter of a million, and he suggested that D'Angelo speak to Danny Motto.

The matter of who was speaking to whom relative to the shaking down of Consolidated Edison soon turned into something of a tangle. It was clearly an idea whose time had come, and a number of approaches were made in 1967. Operators vied in presenting themselves to Itkin, the commissioner's plenipotentiary, with claims that they had an in at the utility; while at Con Edison, the conspirators told one another, there was jockeying going on among vice-presidents who claimed to have an in at the Water Department.

The complications that ensued bespeak a grudging regard even among experienced bribe-passers and arrangers of payoffs for so formidable an institution as Consolidated Edison of New York, the nation's largest supplier of gas and electricity. Our engineers of corruption seem to have shared the ordinary citizen's attitude toward America's great companies. Con Edison may be attacked for its high rates or its unreliable service or the noise of its generators or the smoke from its stacks or its despoilment of nature— all that is appropriate to a great company—but a bribe? One understands that a utility is not above treating with politicians on a certain level (for years Con Edison's executives made certain to take a table at political dinners and other fund-raising affairs, without prejudice as to party affiliation); it may control the votes of state legislators and not even trouble to conceal the strings; it may use its economic powers to squeeze benefits from the localities on which it chooses to impose a steam plant. Such arrangements are within the scope of a great company—but a cold bribe? And if a bribe . . . then to whom? What can any single executive in a great company promise? Which promises can he fulfill?

It fell to Antonio Corallo, whose experience of the world did not abound in men, whatever their station, who could not be bought, to make the first move toward establishing communications with Con Edison. As his professional kinsman, the New Jersey Mafiosi captain Angelo (Gyp) DeCarlo, has stated the principle: "Everybody can be made." Late in 1966, Tony Ducks thought he had someone who could "reach" the utility's top management and arrange for contracts to go to firms willing to kick back part of their profits to the combine. This did not work out, but early in 1967 he notified Itkin, with whom he was meeting several times a week, that he had a more promising candidate: "Now I have arranged with Danny [Motto] to introduce you to someone who can really get to Con Ed." Corallo promised Itkin that if he cooperated with this new man, "we will make good money because there are several contractors that I have and I want to push."

The selected intermediary between the cabal and the utility was Milton Lipkins, who, with his two brothers, ran the Broadway Maintenance Company. Itkin was introduced to Lipkins early in 1967 by Daniel Motto. The introduction took place in the office of a politically well acquainted lawyer named Sam Roman, former Republican assemblyman for Washington Heights, executive assistant to State Attorney General Louis Lefkowitz, and executive secretary of the State Harness Racing Commission. It was Roman who first brought together those two horse lovers, Carl D'Angelo and Daniel Motto.

For several decades Broadway Maintenance had serviced the city's traffic lights, parking meters, and air-raid sirens, and now the brothers Lipkins were seeking a substantial increase in their annual contract. They got the increase and, swears Itkin, he, Marcus, and Motto shared a kickback of almost $28,000. A part of this sum was paid, unprofessionally and inconveniently, by check. According to Itkin, "Sidney Lipkins is the one that complicated the deal because he changed it from cash to check. He said he could only pay four percent by check, one percent in cash, and then Milton said, 'Now my brother really did us a favor. We have these checks between this company and you. We got to do something to cover it up.'" The coverup, relates Itkin, consisted of his presenting bills to Broadway Maintenance for imaginary services in the Dominican

131

Republic: "Milton Lipkins asked that these bills be sent because instead of paying us by cash he paid me by check, and subsequent to the time he paid me by check, he became worried that now there was a check between us. He said, 'You have been making trips to the Dominican. I want the bills because we have to cover up.' " Itkin claims that he shared the Broadway Maintenance money with his partner, clearing only $5,000 or $7,000 for himself, whereas Marcus says that though he would have been perfectly willing to accept a five-percent payoff from the Lipkins brothers on city contracts, he received nothing from this deal, and indeed was unaware of it until an assistant district attorney showed him the canceled checks from Broadway Maintenance made out to Itkin. (No indictments have been brought in this case.)

As contractual guardians of the city's lighting for many years, the principals at Broadway Maintenance found it necessary to maintain contacts in and around City Hall. According to the State Investigations Commission, which issued charges of "extensive irregularities," "inadequate performance," and "excessive profits" against Broadway Maintenance in 1961, when it was entrusted with more than $5.7 million in city contracts, the company regularly allocated $50,000 a year to the purchase of Christmas gifts, such as television sets and "fancy smoked turkeys" for city officials and employees. According to the state investigators, at least two Democrats with intimate political connections in city departments that gave out contracts to Broadway Maintenance had been hired by the company after contracts were received. For seventeen years in a row, Broadway Maintenance had submitted the winning low bid for lighting contracts in Manhattan, the Bronx, and Staten Island, while a "competitor" from Philadelphia had made the low bid for Brooklyn and Queens. It struck the investigators as noteworthy that not once during that whole time had either company submitted a low bid to take over the territory of the other.

Mayor Robert Wagner dismissed the state commission's conclusion that the city was being overcharged $2 million annually, as a political maneuver in an election year. Three city commissioners were pressed into the defense of the lighting contractors, whom state investigators had found to be tampering with their books in order to mislead the city as to their costs of operation. Foremost in the defense was none other than the Commissioner of Water Supply, Gas and Electricity, Armand D'Angelo. He called the charges "exaggerated and irresponsible," and the state commission's conclusions "impractical, unfeasible, and in practically all cases entirely invalid." He defended Broadway Maintenance in words that have served many companies' public-relations departments: the construction and maintenance of street lights, pointed out the commissioner, was "a highly technical and skilled specialty which requires an enormous capital investment."

The Lipkins brothers, alert businessmen, did not confine their commercial adventures to their own company. In 1954, according to another report by the State Investigations Commission (this time confirmed by a city investigation), Sidney Lipkins, the company's president, and his two brothers were partners in a combine that bought 150 undeveloped acres in Queens for the construction of an FHA-guaranteed housing project. In the course of setting up the deal, the investors paid $75,000 to an outfit called City-Wide Servicing Corporation. City-Wide's function

133

was to collect fees on behalf of a couple of the borough's Republican politicos, in return, presumably, for assistance to builders in quest of FHA loans and an understanding attitude by overseers of the city's building codes. The investors obtained a $2.7 million FHA mortgage on their land near Jamaica Bay which they had purchased for $330,000.

So the Lipkins brothers were not unacquainted with the way of the world, or at least of the municipality. Moreover, by the nature of their enterprise, they found themselves in contact with officials of Consolidated Edison. Itkin testified that after the alleged payoff for the rate increase, Milton Lipkins declared that he intended to get back the money. The vehicle was to be Con Edison. Here, in Itkin's summary, was the Lipkins strategy: "Listen, Herb, the real money in Marcus's department is with Con Ed. Everything else is minor when you take into account Con Edison, and you have to really push these people in Con Edison in order to get yourself placed in the right position to get all of their contracts. There is millions and millions of dollars' worth of contracts and that is what everybody shoots for and we have a great shot here if you have the commissioner and he has to listen to what we say. He has to be tough, he can't give them anything. He can just ignore them when they come up to the office, as best he can, and let them get the word that they are not going to get anything from the City of New York—and they need desperately many things from the City of New York. When that occurs, we will pick out contractors; we will have millions of dollars' worth of contracts that we will place with the right contractors and the kickbacks is what we are going to share, and each of these contractors will kick back a great percentage of their money and profit to us."

"Fine," said Itkin, who was by now dreaming of a $5 million payoff from Storm King contractors, and in the weeks that followed, Lipkins reported periodically on his progress, with injunctions to keep the commissioner "tough." By June 1967, Itkin felt able to alert Edward Orlando, who had already shown palpable gratitude for emergency contracts, to the new prospects: "Ed, I hear from someone who is making contact with Con Ed, and I will be able to pick out the contractors to get large contracts from Con Edison. Now, they want to know if I give them to you, will you kick back money for getting the contracts."

"I'll be glad to," said Edward Orlando.

Three other firms were in line for these contracts. Two had made their peace with Antonio Corallo, and the third was associated with Broadway Maintenance. In June, Itkin relates, Milton Lipkins came to him with heartening news: "Look, I think I am really making headway. I have Max Ulrich, who is vice-president of Con Edison, and I think he is going to be either the executive vice-president or the president, and he is my man, and it is pretty well set up."

Max M. Ulrich, forty-two years old in 1967, was Consolidated Edison's vice-president for public relations. He had been with the company for nine years and has been described by a colleague as a man with "a sixth sense about where the centers of power lie." Ulrich had met Milton Lipkins in 1963 or 1964, when Lipkins was associated with

Sydney Baron's public-relations firm. Baron, best known as a confidant of Carmine De Sapio, was retained as a "consultant" to Con Edison, a relationship that was maintained through 1967. Ulrich explains his function: "Mr. Baron's primary work for our company was in public-relations consulting. There are many matters that come up in the life of a big corporation that involve their relationships with the public, and I was the senior officer in the company with that responsibility, and it is helpful—many firms find it helpful to have outside consultants who can advise them, talk over problems, talk over reactions to situations." Baron's close acquaintanceship with political powers in New York could not have detracted from his value as a talker-over of problems with the utility executives.

Early in June, Milton Lipkins called Ulrich with the suggestion that they get together for lunch. They met at the Colony, and we have Ulrich's version of the conversation. After expressing his "great affection" for Con Edison and his sadness over the small amount of work that Broadway Maintenance was doing for the beloved utility, he got around to Con Edison's relations with the Department of Water Supply, Gas and Electricity. "Then Mr. Lipkins said that he had heard our relationships were very bad and that this concerned him; he had been interested in the company and certainly wanted to see it go ahead, and he thought that these relationships certainly needed improvement. . . . He had some friends who were close to the Department of Water Supply, and he thought that if some arrangement could be made whereby a construction company named Orlando could be given, obviously on some preferential basis, a continuing amount of Con Edison's construction business, that this would work to improve our relationship with the Department of Water Supply."

"What do you mean, a sizable portion of the construction business?" asked Ulrich. "Are you talking five or ten percent?" Lipkins indicated that was about what he had in mind, and Ulrich relayed their conversation to Charles E. Eble, then chairman of the board and the utility's chief executive officer.

Not a week passed through the summer of 1967 that Milton Lipkins omitted to call or meet with Max Ulrich to inquire as to Orlando's fortunes. In July at the Baroque Restaurant, Lipkins joined Ulrich and Sydney Baron for lunch. Ulrich recalls: "I actually was having one of my luncheons with Mr. Baron on that date. He and I had planned to meet for lunch, and Mr. Lipkins called up and said he wanted to talk to me and it was important he saw me. And I said, 'Well, look, I am having lunch with Mr. Baron. If you want to join us, I see nothing wrong with that.' So we had lunch that day at the Baroque, which is somewhere in the East Fifties. And Mr. Lipkins came to that luncheon and asked me if I had any answer on this matter about which he had spoken. I said I did not. As I recall, Mr. Lipkins left fairly early in the luncheon, and Mr. Baron and I continued our discussion until maybe one-thirty." How much of what Baron and Ulrich discussed until one-thirty was related to Lipkins's campaign, we do not know, but Baron's own interest in the matter would soon make itself felt.

Milton Lipkins's tactics throughout are clear enough. He had lighted on Ulrich not because the vice-president for public relations had the power to grant contracts at a whim but because Ulrich happened to be the Con Edison vice-president whom Lipkins knew best. He kept pushing the Orlando matter because he needed to demonstrate to Itkin-Corallo that he could come up with results, to their joint profit.

But why should Vice-President Ulrich, doubtless a busy man, have borne with his naggings for all those weeks? And why should he have kept stringing Lipkins along? There is no testimony that Ulrich received any payment for his patience, yet in the fall of 1967, at Lipkins's behest, he interceded in behalf of N. A. Orlando for a pending job. When the $120,000 contract was awarded, Ulrich called Lipkins with the news "that Orlando had won the bid." Why should Ulrich have so condescended? One explanation—his own—is that Orlando, eager for work, was willing to do the job at a bargain price, and it was kind of Milton Lipkins to tip off Con Ed. In reporting Lipkins's offers of mediation and assistance up the chain of command, Ulrich maintains that he was acting in the best interests of his company. Another explanation—favored by Itkin and his cronies—was that Ulrich was using Lipkins's claimed influence at the Water Department to advance his own ambitions within Con Edison. The favor to Orlando could be taken by the plotters as a sign that Lipkins had made his point with Ulrich, who had made the point with his fellow executives, who were now prepared to reach an understanding with Marcus.

Itkin interpreted all this for Marcus at the time that the favor was being done: "Right now there's a power play in there [Con Edison]. Everybody will make their moves, and you gotta go carefully. Now, our man [Ulrich] is right, and Luce [the new board chairman] has now said to Ulrich, 'Max Ulrich, can you do the job?'" Whether

Itkin invented this scene or got it from Lipkins, or whether Lipkins invented it or got it from Ulrich, or whether Ulrich invented it, is unsettled. According to company spokesmen, the Lipkins episode and its exposure did no injury to Max Ulrich's career with Consolidated Edison. In July 1969 he assumed the important post of vice-president for Brooklyn operations, as well as for central customers service, at an increase in salary.

TEN

The Company Man

"I took it."
GERALD R. HADDEN, *former vice-
president of construction,
Consolidated Edison Company
of New York*

Soon after Milton Lipkins opened his campaign against Con Edison on the Ulrich front, persistent Henry Fried put it to Itkin that he, Fried, ought to be directing the Con Edison strategy. At the August meeting with Itkin and Edward Orlando at the Hotel Commodore, where Fried unveiled his silent partnership with the smaller contractor, he told Itkin, "I know just what you are doing with Lipkins and I know what you are doing with Ulrich, and you are just messing it up. . . . I have been in it for many, many years, Herbie. I know what I am telling you, and you fellows are just innocents compared to these things, and I am far from innocent."

Fried was not an easy man for Itkin to put off. He had considerable force of personality, a native gift perhaps or perhaps bred into him during his many years of kneeing and gouging for advantage in the contractors' arena. He was a street fighter grown powerful, and what he lacked in refinement, he made up for with real toughness—as well as with a fortifying consciousness of his own wealth and connections. He was no shrewder than Itkin and probably not as intelligent; but he was much tougher. Moreover, having made one substantial payoff, he could not readily be dismissed from the ongoing game, despite that irksome discrepancy of $11,600. "Eddie," Itkin says he told Orlando when Orlando asked him to meet Fried at the Commodore, "I don't know why you are tying up with Fried. You know it is very difficult for me to deal with Henry Fried because he hasn't completed the other deal." Yet, in truth, Itkin was nothing if not prepared to deal, and the faintest glow of hundreds of thousands of dollars in bribes was sufficient to reconcile him even to slow-paying Fried.

However, he still had the uncomfortable job of explaining Fried's entrance into the Con Edison negotiations to Antonio Corallo, a man whose profession required that a grudge not be lightly relinquished. By the summer of 1967 Corallo was growing impatient at the lagging talks with Con Edison, which the conspirators had had on their collective mind since 1966. At a meeting in July, Corallo and Itkin joined in the following colloquy:

CORALLO: "You know, I don't understand you guys. I had one contract that was supposed to bring in forty-some-odd thousand dollars, and it brings in thirty. Now you have been talking about Con Edison for six months. Where's the money, Herbie? Where's the money?"

ITKIN: "I am doing everything everybody asks me to do, and it doesn't seem to come through. You have to be patient."

CORALLO: "Never mind patient. I am giving the orders. I want the used metal."

ITKIN: "What do you mean, used metal?"

CORALLO: "Con Ed has enormous amounts of used copper—and here is the deal. It has been going on for years, and now it is my deal. I have notified everybody, and you

141

better see I get it. I want to buy used copper, and I will bid high for the used copper, but somebody in Con Ed better get the word when my truck comes in, if we bid for a thousand pounds, we take out five thousand pounds, and somebody better close their eyes to it. That is the way we can bid high, get the bid, and make the money—and you get the word to the commissioner, or whoever else, I want this and I want it now. I am tired of waiting for you guys. It is just a game you are playing like a bunch of screwballs."

ITKIN: "I will tell the commissioner—and I am telling you we are trying."

CORALLO: "Never mind trying. Just do it."

Later, when Itkin could no longer conceal Henry Fried's entrance, with Orlando, into the maneuverings around Con Edison, he put the news this way: "Orlando is going to tie in with Fried so Fried doesn't bid against him on any of this. Now, I don't want to meet Fried and I told him. I refused fifteen times, and so did Jim. We met them once and that was it. I said I am not dealing with Henry Fried, and that was that."

That, however, was not quite that. Although it was desirable, for peace of mind all around, that Tony Ducks be mollified, it could not be accomplished at Henry Fried's expense. Even making allowances for Fried's tendency to flaunt his influence with useful personages, his connections at Con Edison were much more solid than those of Milton Lipkins. Whereas Broadway Maintenance's work for the utility amounted only to a few thousand dollars a year, Fried's firms had annual contracts in the millions, making Fried one of Con Edison's principal contractors. In addition to a considerable amount of excavation and

construction work, his companies had the contract to remove ashes from some generating plants and, as we have
already noted, sold the output of the utility's fly-ash sin-
tering plant* to builders. In the course of carrying out
these activities over a number of years, Fried had not
failed to build up relationships with high utility executives,
several of whom had enjoyed his hospitality. The relationship that held out the greatest promise in the second half
of 1967, for him and for Marcus-Itkin, was with Gerald R.
Hadden.

In 1967 Gerald Hadden was fifty-seven years old. He
had gone to work for Consolidated Edison in 1931, fresh
out of school, and had made his way up the company
ladder. In 1958 he became vice-president of construction.
By 1967 his salary was $51,000 a year, plus perquisites ap-
propriate to his station, such as a car and chauffeur. Hadden's responsibilities covered power plants, substations,
and street work: "My job was to get the structures built."
It was a job that invited the attention of contractors.

Around 1966 the head of Slattery Contracting, one of the
largest firms in its field, doing upwards of two million dollars' work each year for Con Edison (and many times that
amount for the state), sold Vice-President Hadden 250
shares of Slattery stock. Hadden's name did not appear in
the transaction, and he paid for the shares in cash—a dollar a share. He divided the stock between his two daugh-
ters, and soon afterwards Slattery Contracting bought it
all back, for $15,000—a brisk profit to the Hadden family
of $14,750. In the fall of 1966 Mr. and Mrs. Hadden took a

* *Sinter*—to cause to become a coherent, non-porous mass by heating
without melting.

143

trip to Europe with the president of Slattery and his wife. The contractor paid for the Haddens' airline tickets and for part of their hotel accommodations. Asked whether he had ever received anything besides the $15,000 from Slattery, Hadden explained, "I took a trip with him. I didn't consider that giving anything."

The question of what Gerald Hadden considered to be "giving" has its interesting side. So much has been written in dispraise of the organization man that he is no longer fit subject for abuse. Yet there is one quality—not touched with nobility, yet not without worth—that we may still expect of him: loyalty to the company that has raised him so high, the company to which he owes all his physical comforts as well as whatever inner security he has been able to develop over the decades. Yet here was a vice-president of a most imposing and reputedly paternal organization taking favors for . . . for what? Hadden denies that he ever used his high station to earn the kindnesses of Slattery's president. If so, it was an unusually sentimental relationship for the business world, as it implies an outlay of capital funds with no prospect of return. But business executives are not known for their powers of introspection, and insofar as Hadden allowed his favor-taking to intrude upon his consciousness, he was probably able to reassure himself that though he took what he could get, from Slattery, from Henry Fried, perhaps from others, in violation of company policy, he never actually *did* anything to hurt Con Edison.

What drew the attention of Henry Fried (and, evidently, the head of Slattery Construction) to Gerald Hadden in 1966 was the death that June of the senior vice-president to whom he had been reporting and with whom

Fried had theretofore done most of his business. Now Hadden, who was in charge of preparing bidding lists from which contractors were drawn for Con Edison projects, began to report directly to the president of the company. Up until 1966, according to Hadden, Fried's Christmas gift would be no more than a case of whisky, but after his superior's death there was dramatic improvement. The two met fairly regularly from June onward; exactly what they discussed remains cloudy, but we know that one of Fried's contracts was up for renewal that July. They apparently struck it off, for that December Fried gave Hadden not a case of whisky but a $1,000 gift certificate to Saks Fifth Avenue. Fried knew his man. They met often in 1967, usually at lunch. After one such lunch, in January, Fried handed Hadden an envelope containing $1,000 in cash.

"What is this for?" Hadden recalls inquiring.

Fried replied, "Take it."

Hadden says that he said, "I don't want it."

"Take it," said Fried.

And he took it.

In February again Fried gave Hadden an envelope; and again it was found to contain $1,000. Again, says Hadden, he said he didn't want to take it. Again he took it. Between January and September of 1967 Hadden had $7,500 thus forced upon him by Fried. He was now on Henry Fried's payroll.

In addition to the pending plans regarding Storm King, there were a number of other uses to which a man such as Fried might put a man such as Hadden. The vice-president of construction was a nonpareil source of information about upcoming projects, and we may be certain that Fried pumped him. As the executive in charge of compiling bidding lists, Hadden was the natural official to receive Fried's complaints about an extension of those lists, early in 1967, to include some twelve potential contractors instead of about eight. Their conversation on this subject, as Hadden relates it, was excruciatingly proper.

Fried cautioned: "You are going to get people who will not perform the work the way we are performing it if you go out and get some of these unqualified people."

Hadden replied: "The company policy is to extend the list, and we are going to try to find people who can do this work the way we want it done."

Not the sort of exchange that one would expect between benefactor and beneficiary, but there seems to have been little that Hadden could do about the new policy on bidding lists, and Fried had to carry his arguments to Con Edison's administrative vice-president, who interpreted them as "just a complaint that he was not making enough money and this really made him very unhappy."

(As it happens, Henry Fried was master of another method of beating the nuisance of competitive bidding— an arrangement among contractors to rig their bids for paving and trenching contracts with Con Edison, with the Brooklyn Union Gas Company, and with the Empire City Subway Company, a subsidiary of the New York Telephone Company. In October 1969, Fried was sentenced to four months in jail and fined $25,000 for his role in this accommodation; Mackay Construction was fined $50,000; and S. T. Grand was fined $10,000.) *

* Henry Fried's fellow conspirators, a list of the city's contractor nobility, included: Vincent P. DiNapoli, chairman of Tully & DiNapoli;

Vice-President Hadden was able to serve Henry Fried better in another matter that whetted the appetite of that remarkably hungry man. In September 1967, Fried bought two old two-story buildings adjacent to a Con Edison installation on 111th Street, near First Avenue, in Manhattan. Hadden swears that he learned of the purchase only when Fried told him he would like to sell the buildings to Con Edison. It seemed to Hadden that they were conveniently situated for the utility's use, and he suggested that Fried take his offer to the administrative vice-president; he did so, with Hadden interceding in his behalf. At first Chairman Luce said no to the purchase, but Hadden persisted. Early in October, a very few weeks after Fried had taken title to the property—for $120,000, he says—Con Edison leased the building from him for $1,250 a month. Not a major item in the accounts of a multimillionaire, but Fried seemed to get a special kick out of this sort of inside arrangement; he prided himself on knowing whom to reach, and how. His good humor over the lease was tangibly expressed at his October luncheon meeting with Gerald Hadden. Fried handed Hadden an envelope which contained not the customary $1,000 but

---

Francis Jordan, board chairman of Poirier & McLane; Alfred Korsen, executive vice-president of Slattery Contracting; Theodore Galucci, Jr., president of Samuel Galucci & Sons; Joseph J. Haggerty, Sr., board chairman of Sicilian Asphalt Paving; Samuel Aviron, superintendent of Lipsett, Inc.; Robert Crimmins, president of Thomas Crimmins Contracting; Arthur Cipolla, vice-president of Yonkers Contracting; Robert E. Lee, secretary of DeLee General Construction; and Ernest Muccini, Sr., president of Oakhill Contracting. Two other companies were in on the bid-rigging: Gull Contracting of Queens, and Casper Helock of the Bronx. The price-fixing companies are still handling the bulk of Con Edison's $30-million-a-year worth of trenching, paving, and foundation work. Explains Chairman Luce, "These firms are among the largest in the city and there simply are not enough other qualified contractors staffed and equipped to do the job."

$2,500, saying, "This is your commission." Honest old Bishop Latimer cried, "Leave coloring, and call these things by their Christian name, bribes!"

It was in October, too, that Fried gave Hadden to understand that he wanted N. A. Orlando favored for work that Con Edison had to have done in connection with a city water-supply tunnel south of Fourteenth Street. It was the same job about which Milton Lipkins had approached Max Ulrich—and, as already reported, Orlando got it.

Fried's payments to Hadden were as much in expectation as in gratitude. Their association continued until December 1967, when exposure overtook the bedraggled conspiracy. Early in 1968 Hadden was relieved of his duties at Con Edison and given the alternative of resigning or retiring. He chose to retire, eight years before normal retirement age, and on February 1 he severed his lifetime connection with the utility, at a cut-rate pension. He took a new position with a firm that had done electrical work for Con Edison for many years.

Hadden's forced exit from Con Edison was unusual. Even when management consultants make their expensive studies and report that the utility is top heavy with executives, no one's job is put at hazard. That helps to account not only for the excessive number of executives employed by Con Edison over the years but for their famously undistinguished quality. The forced departure of Gerald Hadden was Con Edison's way of notifying us that his case was highly unusual, even unique. That up until his time no vice-president had enjoyed favors from contractors, beyond a case of whisky at Christmas. That until the president of Slattery found Hadden, he had no one. That until Henry Fried found Hadden, he was constrained to straightforward dealings with the utility. Hadden, taking his reduced pension and going his way, thus served his company to the end. As for his ready acceptance by a kindred firm, there is nothing sinister or even abnormal in that. Friendship requires no less, and it is not unlikely that, once removed from temptation, the susceptible company man will be able to do the job for his new company.

But we have run ahead of our story. The summer of 1967 found the conspirators—Marcus-Itkin, Fried, Corallo, Orlando, Lipkins, and others—maneuvering on various fronts but making no progress toward the pot of gold up at Storm King. All parties were impatient, and none more so than the self-confident, hard-driving Fried. But he had jollier matters to occupy his mind that summer. Sunday, August 20, a day of drizzle as it turned out, was set for the opening of Clermont, his extravagant new horse farm at Germantown, New York, about a hundred miles up the Hudson River from the city. Contributing to Fried's high spirits that day was the recent approval by the New York City Board of Estimate of an increase of $468,247 on an S. T. Grand contract for cleaning and repairing the water lines in the East New York section of Brooklyn. The improvement in the original price, from $708,243 to $1,176,490, "for additional work," was requested by Commissioner Marcus. The commissioner did not attend the party, nor did Gerald Hadden, but Max Ulrich dropped in, on his way to Montreal's Expo '67: "It was quite a gala day." Itkin was there too: "Oh, it was a very large affair. They had tents and orchestras and several places where you could get drinks and all sorts of food being cooked. There must have been a thousand people there."

Itkin had been asked to the party for something more than the sheer fun of it. He was at his table with the Orlandos when Fried beckoned him away: "There is somebody I want you to meet." They left the tent and walked over to a waiting figure whom Itkin had no difficulty recognizing. "Carmine," said Fried to his friend of twenty years, "this is Herbert Itkin, who I told you about. Now, I have talked to both of you independently about what I'd like. I will do my end if the two of you can work together."

"Fine," said Itkin.

"Well, I may be interested in working with you," said Carmine De Sapio, "but I want it understood that you work with no one else at all if I work with you. I want that clear, that I don't want other people in it. I don't think you have been handling yourself well at all."

ELEVEN

The Boss

"Carmine knows what he is doing."
Antonio Corallo

THE function and reputation of the political boss have changed somewhat since Lord Bryce examined the phenomenon in the last century. The boss no longer does so much of his work in his city's saloons, and his scope has been circumscribed, his techniques refined by periodic reforms. Much of the flamboyance has been taken out of the role. Yet he exists still, if in reduced circumstances, and the reason for his existence is not so different from what it was in more robust times. Bryce's summation applies today as it did nearly a hundred years ago: "The aim of a Boss is not so much fame as power, and not so much power over the conduct of affairs as over persons. Patronage is the sort of power he seeks, patronage understood in the largest sense in which it covers the disposal of lucrative contracts and other modes of enrichment as well as salaried places. The dependents who surround him desire wealth, or at least a livelihood; his business is to find this for them, and in doing so he strengthens his own position. It is as the bestower of riches that he holds his position, like the leader of a band of condottieri in the fifteenth century."

The reference to the condottieri approaches prophecy. Young Carmine G. De Sapio's conquest of New York City's Tammany organization in the late nineteen-thirties and early forties was a victory for the wave of Italian immigrants that had succeeded the immigrant Irish onto these shores. Out went Danny Finn, third of his name to rule the Lower West Side of Manhattan; in came Carmine De Sapio to begin a career that would bring him control of the city, overriding political power in the state, and, for an hour, a voice in the country's affairs. His greatest years came in the middle nineteen-fifties when he successfully backed Robert Wagner for mayor and then W. Averell Harriman for governor. He ruled the city's Democratic organization, became Governor Harriman's secretary of state (and was responsible in this role for turning his good friend and contributor Henry Fried into a commissioner of correction—a minor gaffe, when we remember that as sheriff of Bronx County, Ed Flynn swore in Dutch Schultz as an honorary deputy), and was New York's Democratic national committeeman. His decline began in 1958, when, against the wishes of both Harriman and Wagner, he got the Democratic senatorial nomination for Frank Hogan, New York's enduring district attorney. An odd project for a politician who had enjoyed the sponsorship of Frank Costello, and a Pyrrhic victory—Hogan was beaten and carried on as district attorney, but De Sapio never recovered. New York's Reform Democratic movement had begun, and in 1961 De Sapio lost the leadership of his own district. ". . . to lose your district in a primary," wrote Norman Thomas and Paul Blanshard in 1932, "is political suicide." De Sapio's official powers were gone, and along with them his power to hand-pick candidates. Yet the aura of influence lingered. He had not been an especially astute political leader, but as party boss he had won a reputation for trustworthiness. That is, having entered into an agreement, he could be counted on to fulfill his part. Now, though dispossessed of titles, he retained his reputation. It was much envied in his circle, but before he was done, it would become most unenviable.

In part, such a reputation comes with the job. Few citizens can say what it is that the political boss spends his days at, but most have a sense that he is busy maneuvering and manipulating—arranging things, trading favors, cooking up deals; and most have no doubt that, through all the maneuvering and manipulating, he personally comes out ahead. Whatever it is that he does, he seems to do wonderfully at it. In the witness chair, Carmine De Sapio was hard put to say how he had made his living between 1939 and 1946, his early years as leader of the First Assembly District, the base upon which he rose in New York Democratic politics. When in 1957 a cab driver found a paper bag containing $11,200 in cash in his back seat shortly after having had De Sapio as a passenger, De Sapio's professions of ignorance brought smiles and wisecracks throughout the city. In the nineteen-fifties, too, he established a connection with an insurance-brokerage firm in New York; by 1969, he claimed, this was his full-time job, for which he received $28,000 a year, plus bonuses. Yet he was not a licensed insurance agent: "I am not an insurance expert, and I don't profess to be. I am an ex-political leader." And what does an ex-political leader do to earn his salary with an insurance firm? "I try to promote good will for the J. B. Rappaport Insurance Company. . . . There is nothing wrong in that." Though the world may snicker, there is nothing wrong in that. And how does one promote such good will? "Primarily through acquaintances that I have acquired over a period of years." The political boss must know everyone in his territory whom it is worth knowing. De Sapio brought with him to Henry Fried's big horse-farm opening in August 1967 his old friend Frank G. Rossetti, who had lately become New York County Democratic leader: "I thought it might be a good opportunity that he meet some of these people." Which people? "The highest-type people in the business and professional world."

No political boss can quite shake loose of the character that he inherits along with the title, and Carmine De Sapio's appearance and manner could only confirm it. No matter how many times he explained that his dark glasses were forced on him by a chronic inflammation of the iris, they still gave him a sinister aspect. He was not one of Lord Bryce's "vulgar figures in good coats"; he dressed soberly, spoke softly, and carried himself with a kind of painful dignity, as though determined to be better than his calling. And indeed he seems to have been better. Yet the reserved bearing and discreet manner only reinforced the common view of him as a shady operator. One got a sense as he testified at his trial of the strain it cost him to project what he hoped would be an un-bosslike image. Asked whether he had played any active role in politics after his last defeat in his own Greenwich Village district in 1965, he answered: "No, I didn't continue any active role, but I would have to frankly admit that my relationships in the political spectrum were such that I would find myself activated only to the extent of attending political functions and dinners, et cetera. That would be the extent of my activation." A man cannot live at ease amid such locutions.

No one believed that the great influence of De Sapio in New York ended with his political overthrow. Diminished it surely was—but he had done too many favors, he had too many friends, he had shared too many confidences to be left out. The persons who drew the most dishonorable conclusions as to De Sapio's current way of life were those, naturally, who were themselves deficient in honor. On one of the tapes of Mafia conversations which filled our newspapers early in 1970, one racketeer is heard saying that another "must have given over half a million" to De Sapio, who "probably stuck a couple of hundred thousand right in his pocket." De Sapio denies acquaintance with any of the parties to this conversation, and in light of the popular weakness for projecting upon others those vices which we know most intimately, the Mafia reference, entirely unsubstantiated, may be disregarded as hearsay of a most slanderous kind; for all we know the Mafia chiefs accept the same stereotype regarding public figures with Italian names as do the rest of us.

Alas, the reputation of Carmine De Sapio, instead of giving the lie to even so casual a charge, could only suffer new smirks from newspaper readers who remembered that in his Tammany days the young and rising politician was favored by Frank Costello. (Nothing singular in that. As another Tammany boss, Hugo Rogers, epitomized the relationship, "If Costello wanted me, he would send for me.") Antonio Corallo, for one, remembered. Itkin tells us that De Sapio was no happier than Henry Fried to learn that types like Corallo and Pizzo had been in on earlier deals, whereas Corallo was fairly bowled over on learning that Itkin had met personally with Carmine De Sapio. "Gee, how come? How come?" the tough guy gushed. And on being told that "He is going to handle everything now," Tony Ducks, who had never gotten close to De Sapio, rose to the rhapsodical: "He sits at his desk, has the matters all arranged for him; when they come to him it is all arranged." Then he delivered himself of this encomium: "Carmine knows what he is doing." Such is the force of reputation.

At his trial, De Sapio would explain away his meetings with Itkin, Hadden, and Ulrich as chance encounters, he personally having no interest in the relations between Consolidated Edison and New York City. By De Sapio's account, Itkin intruded himself at the horse-farm opening: "My name is Herbert Itkin. I don't think you know me, but I know something about you, and if I may for a moment, I would like to talk to you. . . . I'm a good friend of Jim Marcus, the Commissioner of Water Supply, Gas and Electricity. I'm his adviser and his counselor, and Jim, as you have been reading about, has a good political potential, and I think he's going places." According to De Sapio, Itkin bothered him several times after that meeting, seeking such favors as the application of political influence in his suit to regain custody of his second wife's children. (Itkin remains convinced that his wife's first husband has fixed Westchester Family Court.) De Sapio contends that he told Itkin "that I was deactivated politically, and while I would not be adverse to talking to him or anybody else about politics generally, there wasn't anything I could contribute on any political level for his benefit or anyone else's."

Now, substantively as well as stylistically, that's a

mouthful, and difficult to swallow. Still, one may credit De Sapio's version of his meetings with Itkin, as far as it goes. It was entirely in character for the tireless operator to press his attentions on so fabulous a figure as Carmine De Sapio. Itkin shared Corallo's awe at the name, and it was entirely in character for him to ask favors wherever he could ask them. Given his various careers, one can hardly question his talent for telling a good tale, with elaboration where required. Yet Itkin's account of the progress of the Con Edison conspiracy, from August to December of 1967, fits better than De Sapio's with what can be derived from other sources. So concluded the ladies and gentlemen of the jury, and we shall follow their example here.

A few days after the August 20 meeting at the horse farm, Itkin brought the good news back to Marcus:

"Jim, Carmine De Sapio contacted me, and he wants to handle our proposition with Con Ed."

"Great," responded Marcus. "Maybe we can get somewheres now. We haven't been getting anywheres, and Corallo is really pushing us. What are we going to do? Do you think he will get us money fast?"

"You can't push someone like Carmine for money fast."

"Yes, but move him."

"I don't know that I can. You just have to be patient now."

"When are you going to call him?"

"I don't think we ought to look too anxious. Why don't we wait until after Labor Day?"

"All right."

Asked later about his reaction to having included in the conspiracy a man whom he had never met and who apparently had no political influence with the Republican city administration, Marcus replied, "Political influence comes from strange directions." His education was moving right along.

Not every businessman in New York who claimed to have Carmine De Sapio on his payroll could actually produce him in the flesh; this much Henry Fried showed that he could do. Soon after Labor Day, 1967, Itkin called De Sapio, and they met at the Biltmore, where, says Itkin, he received a scolding. Here is his paraphrase of the lecture which De Sapio denies delivering: "Herb, I've checked you fellows out. I think you have made some bad mistakes in the way you are handling yourselves—and, remember, if you want to be in the big leagues with us, we have been doing this for a long time; we know all the ropes, and you have been fumbling around." Toward Itkin's dealings with Mafiosi, he took an avuncular tone: "I am surprised you are tied up with these people. . . . I think you are very foolish to trust these people in any of your deals. You are handling it very wrong." His cardinal error, De Sapio counseled, was to have "let them handle the money. If you don't let them handle the money, you have a chance. If you let them handle the money, you are never going to get your share. I have always been sure to take the position that I myself would handle it." Regarding the matter at hand, De Sapio put Itkin on notice that "I don't want you to do one thing in relation to Con Edison without calling me first. I will not be bothered by your phone calls. You call me as often as you want. Stay on top of the situation. As long as I know everything that is going on, we won't have a problem, but I must know it the minute it happens, and don't take a step, or don't let the commissioner take a step without first contacting me." De Sapio further impressed upon him, says Itkin, that Lipkins-Ulrich were not up to the job at hand, whereas he, puissant Carmine in consort with Vincent Albano, "had almost everything boxed in the city." *

Witness Itkin's recollections of other people's conversations tend to be rich in incriminating statements; they capture the attention like the fruits and nuts in a Christmas pudding, and one may have trouble digesting them as served. Yet even if we put aside some of the richer ingredients, his story holds together. The substance of this early meeting was an outline of a rather sophisticated strategy for getting at Consolidated Edison. In May of 1967 the president of the utility had written to Commissioner Marcus for permission to increase the power in its Westchester aqueduct highline. This twenty-mile, 138,000-volt power line, built in 1932, carried electricity from sources upstate into the city. The use of electricity having increased greatly in thirty-five years, it was Con Edison's desire to increase the capacity of the line. The city had agreed in principle in 1966 to make available avenues for bringing in more power, but now the utility needed approval from the Water Department, since the highline ran above an aqueduct in Westchester County that carried water into New York. The letter of May 1967 had been passed along to the department's engineers in order that they might satisfy themselves that the proposed rebuilding would not dam-

---

* The candid Senator Plunkitt of Tammany Hall explained: "When Tammany's on top, I do good turns for the Republicans. When they're on top, they don't forget me. Me and the Republicans are enemies just one day in the year—election day. Then we fight tooth and nail. The rest of the time it's live and let live with us. . . . You see, we differ on tariffs and currencies and all them things, but we agree on the main proposition that when a man works in politics, he should get something out of it."

age the aqueduct or disturb the water supply, and Con Edison had not yet obtained the required approval.

Itkin had heard something of the highline in August and had asked Marcus to look into its status: ". . . when Mr. Itkin asked me about a highline, I knew he must have something in mind." Now, in September, De Sapio outlined his plan to Itkin: "You know, everybody has been talking to me, and I am sure to you, about Storm King Mountain. Now, that's an enormous project. Maybe a hundred million dollars' worth of construction, and if you want to handle this properly, let's do it in stages. The first thing I want you to do is, we will work on the Westchester highline. It's a much simpler proposition. We will lay the ground rules for Con Ed; we will handle the Westchester highline. Once Con Ed knows they can't deal, and they have to deal with us, we will do the Westchester highline. Once that's done, we will have no trouble on this big contract on Storm King, because then the ground rules are laid. We'll get any one of our contractors we want in, and you won't have any headaches. But you have got to do it my way."

Itkin agreed readily and promised to relay the plan to Marcus. But when he called his friend later that day he learned that, at about the time that he had been chatting with De Sapio, Con Edison's vice-president of engineering had been in the commissioner's office, making inquiry as to why he had received no answer to the May request for approval. The coincidence becomes less surprising when we remember that private lines had been open for some months between the cabal and Con Edison officials. By approaching the commissioner directly, the utility's executives may have been attempting an end run around go-betweens of the ilk of Milton Lipkins. Marcus had not yet divined the part that the highline was supposed to play in his own fortunes, and in response to the visiting vice-president (who, incidentally, had a reputation for honesty), he asked the Water Department's chief engineer why approval had been delayed. Engineer Groopman explained that there was no great problem—but his staff wanted to know more about the proposed location of the new transmission towers in order to make certain that the ground could hold them safely, without danger to the aqueduct.

"Could I have a letter to that effect?" asked the vice-president of Consolidated Edison.

"Yes, you can," said Marcus, and he directed engineer Groopman to prepare such a letter.

On learning that Con Edison had been promised a letter of some sort, Itkin told Marcus to hold off, and immediately called De Sapio. "I am doing just as you asked," he announced. "I am contacting you. My friend said that the thing that you wanted us to work on has already been agreed to."

"What do you mean, 'agreed to'? " asked De Sapio.

"There is a letter going out."

De Sapio was nonplused: "It can't go out. It is much too early for me to make a move to impress upon them they have to come to me, and neither can Henry."

"Well, what is there to do?"

"You just tell him to hold up that letter. This is ridiculous."

Itkin called Marcus and relayed instructions: "Our friend Carmine says no letter." And he added, perhaps with a sigh or a private smile, "You have to be tough."

TWELVE

The Highline

*"When somebody buys an insurance
policy from me, then I have to
see the money is paid."*
CARMINE DE SAPIO,
as quoted by HERBERT ITKIN

THE toughness of James Marcus was a subject of ab-
sorbing interest through the fall of 1967 in various
quarters of Manhattan, including those on Irving Place
occupied by the Consolidated Edison Company. Charles
Luce, who took over as chairman of Con Edison's board of
trustees and the company's chief executive officer on August 1, 1967 (annual salary, before taxes, $150,000, plus
$50,000 in "deferred compensation"), was not privy to all
the ramifications of the relationships which his predecessor and subordinates maintained with such parties as
Henry Fried, Carmine De Sapio, and Milton Lipkins, but
he was soon made aware of the problems being caused by
the city's delay in granting its permission to proceed with
work along the aqueduct right-of-way. Contracts amounting to some $6 million were pending for the relocation of
strategic facilities in Westchester County prior to the rebuilding of the transmission line, scheduled to begin in
October 1967. Luce felt that he could not award these
contracts until he had in hand a letter from Commissioner
Marcus containing a firm assurance that the city did not
object to the project. From September on, the pursuit of

this letter was a recurring item on the crowded agenda of the utility's managers.

Charles Luce tells us that he had no knowledge of any private efforts by Vice-Presidents Hadden and Ulrich, but Itkin seems to have been under the impression that considerable pushing and pulling was going on in the executive suite. His predisposition to a faith in the Big Fix was apparently nourished in this instance by the reports he was receiving from Lipkins, whose mission was actually in the throes of failure, and from De Sapio, who was acquainted with a number of important Con Edison officials, notably Luce's predecessor as board chairman, Charles Eble. (Eble continued his association with the utility for several months after Luce's arrival, becoming chairman of the company's executive committee.) Itkin would tell his colleagues, "Luce went back to Max Ulrich, and he says, 'Max, Eble says he can do it and he has the commissioner.'" Perhaps Itkin was merely attempting to pacify the edgy Corallo, or perhaps he was himself misled. Whatever the tactics being employed at Con Edison, the focus was on James Marcus—though even the most experienced, most cynical executives could not have appreciated the breadth of his susceptibility—and he found himself under increasingly heavy pressures in the autumn of his last year as a municipal official.

On receiving Itkin's injunction early in September against sending out any letters, Marcus resolved on a delaying tactic that he hoped would provide the time needed for De Sapio to arrange everything to everyone's advantage. He took the draft letter of approval to the city's Corporation Counsel, where he assumed it would languish for a while. "To the best of my knowledge," says Chairman

Luce, "the request for a permit to rebuild the highline is the only permit that was referred to the Corporation Counsel's office."

But the official there did not grasp what was desired of him. Marcus explained: "I want to send the letter, and I want you to add something so they won't go ahead and rely on it, and go ahead with it."

"Okay," said the corporation counsel; and right there, as Marcus looked haplessly on, a paragraph was added absolving the city from any commitments undertaken by Con Edison regarding contracts for work on the highline.

Marcus was surprised by such a show of bureaucratic efficiency: "I had thought that I would give it to him, and it would take two or three weeks before he would get around to it. But he did it while I was seated there."

He reported wanly back to Itkin on this startling turn, adding, "Well, the letter now doesn't mean very much because they can't spend any money in reliance on the letter."

But Itkin, coached by De Sapio, was adamant: "It doesn't matter whether it means much or not. Don't send the letter!"

"All right," said Marcus, and he explained that he now intended to take it to the city's Director of Franchises: "He will start negotiating." By resolving on this step, it would turn out, Commissioner Marcus was inadvertently acting in behalf of the city's taxpayers, thereby lending weight to Montaigne's observation that deceit has its place in the world.

Within a day or two of the writing of the undelivered letter, Marcus's father died in Schenectady, and Marcus left New York for a week. He returned on September 18, barely in time to prepare for a meeting with the mayor and Con Edison chairman Charles Luce at Gracie Mansion. The meeting was held on September 19. The two potentates of Metropolis exchanged greetings and talked in a general way about subjects of mutual concern. As they concluded, Luce asked Marcus, whom he found to be a "solemn, sad-eyed fellow," whether the two of them might chat on for a few minutes. The city was beset by one of its teachers' strikes at the time and Gracie Mansion was bustling. So they went outside and sat on a bench on the lawn. After agreeing that engineers from the city and from the utility ought to get together to discuss whether the proposed Storm King project might interfere with New York's water supply, Luce directed the conversation to the highline: "I recalled for Commissioner Marcus that the city and the company had entered into an agreement in 1966, whereby the company agreed to build power plants outside the City of New York in an effort to reduce air pollution from power plants, and the city, on its part, had agreed to make available whatever avenues it could make available to bring the power from these power plants located outside the city into the city where it could be used. I then called to his attention the fact that the company had applied for permission to rebuild and enlarge the capacity of one of these transmission lines in Westchester County, which was an essential part of the transmission system to bring the power in from these new power plants we were building in Westchester County pursuant to our understanding with the city."

Marcus admitted to being rather vague about the highline. It was his understanding, he said, that the city's engineers were waiting for Con Edison to supply geological data obtained from core drillings where each of the new transmission poles would be set up, in order to make sure that the ground could take them safely, without jeopardy to the aqueduct below.

Luce promised to check with his engineers. In the meantime he renewed the request for a letter approving the project. Now, a direct request from the chairman of the board of Consolidated Edison to a municipal official is no light matter. The utility is a major force in the city, keeping its high-power transmission lines to important politicians in good repair. Moreover, at the time of the Gracie Mansion conversation the blackout that had struck the city in November 1965 was still unnervingly present in the public mind, and it ill became a city official to put roadblocks in the path of a more secure power supply— to be provided in a manner that would pollute some other part of the country than the amply polluted city, a great step forward ecologically. If another blackout should strike, Chairman Luce could be counted on to point the finger of blame at City Hall. Marcus, perhaps conscious of these considerations, perhaps moved by the realization that Luce had direct access to the mayor, perhaps merely out of a habit of bowing to strength, said yes, he might be able to send along the desired letter. And, in fact, he updated to September 21 the letter which had been prepared but not sent a couple of weeks earlier, and readied it for mailing.

On September 20, according to Itkin, he and Carmine De Sapio had lunch at the Biltmore. De Sapio concedes that they met but denies that it was for lunch or that the meeting had been set up in advance or that Con Edison was mentioned in any way, shape, or form. Itkin, he says, sought him out at the Biltmore, talked him into sitting down for a few minutes for a cup of coffee, and broached the possibility that he might help De Sapio get in on housing-mortgage insurance for the state or city.

Itkin's version of the meeting is different. De Sapio, he says, voiced perplexity about Marcus: "I don't quite understand the commissioner, and I would like to get some background on him. What is this pressure that Henry told me about?"

"Carmine," Itkin says he replied, skirting his own role in Marcus's difficulties, "he is in such a swindle over a stock venture and he can't bail himself out and he's desperate for money. He has all sorts of people bothering him on some stock deal and the stock is just dropping—the bottom has dropped out of it and he's lost and he can't make it up, and this is why he is willing to do what he's doing. But he has to get the money, and it's just being delayed and delayed and no money is coming over."

"Well, what type of man is Commissioner Marcus?" asked Carmine De Sapio.

"I think he's really good. I think he was just wild and thought he was going to make millions. He wants money, and big money. . . . He just got himself trapped."

From Itkin's description, it seemed to De Sapio that Marcus was "pretty irresponsible." Still, in consideration of the young man's plight, he thought he could arrange for a $25,000 payoff on the highline. "Why don't you get back to him and tell him that and just be patient a little while longer. I think we are making the right moves, but you have to understand that in this type of matter we have to be very sophisticated about the way we are doing it. We have to have Con Ed so hungry and so much against the wall that they are willing to accept any help, and then when I come in I can impress upon them. But if the commissioner is telling you he is being tough, that is not the word I get. He is sort of dealing with them, and he is not making it clear. He is making my job just that much more difficult."

The next day Itkin called Marcus, mainly to bring him up to date on a possible arrangement with Brooklyn Union Gas, servicers of Brooklyn and Queens. De Sapio had asked whether Itkin would be interested in taking a large "public-relations contract" with the company. But Marcus felt that it wasn't a sound idea: "We are too close, and everybody in the city knows we are close. For you to have your name on a contract with Brooklyn Union Gas is almost like throwing it in their faces." Itkin concurred—anyway, the idea of paying taxes on the income offended him.

During this conversation, Itkin was startled to learn that Marcus was, again and despite all injunctions, preparing to send out a letter to Con Edison.

"No letters!" Itkin pounded in the point. "No letters at all!"

"Well, it's very difficult," pleaded Marcus.

Itkin stood fast: "Jim, then get out of it. Either you are going to play the game or you are not going to play the game. I tell you, everybody has told me, Lipkins has told me, now De Sapio has told me: 'No letters!' Now, if you don't want to listen, tell me now."

"No," Marcus yielded. "I will listen. I will do anything you want."

Whereupon Itkin added to their scheme a touch that surely tickled his conspiratorial soul. The day before, De

Sapio had suggested that it would be prudent if, when leaving messages, they referred to one another as "Mr. Carl" and "Mr. Herbert." Now Itkin told Marcus that when he got the okay from De Sapio on the Con Edison letter, he would relay it in code, saying: "Will you please send the letter to my niece Plumps in England." (Itkin actually had a niece of that name in England.)

Marcus saw nothing amusing about this device, whatever criticial judgment he once possessed having been mauled by two years of Itkin's plots, and he was pleased to learn that he would be getting some money. There is a disagreement about how much Itkin promised Marcus. Itkin maintains that he intended to give his friend $10,000 of the promised $25,000 and share the balance with De Sapio. Marcus understood that the $10,000 was to be divided between himself and Itkin. One is left to mull over the possibility that Itkin was planning to split $15,000 of Henry Fried's payoff with De Sapio and then split $10,-000 with Marcus.

When could he expect the money, asked the commissioner. And Itkin replied bluntly: "When you don't send letters and you don't promise letters."

Nothing could come less easily to Marcus's temperament than resistance to the pressures that were beating at him from several directions. Late Friday afternoon, September 22, when the last mail delivery had been distributed at Con Edison, he received a call from Chairman Luce: "Where's the letter?"

Marcus explained that another problem had come up, in addition to that of the test core samples. Now, he said, Con Edison's franchise to run its lines above the city's aqueduct would have to be renegotiated. The city wanted more money from the utility, he said, because of the great increase in power to be run through the new lines. The discussion, heated at moments, ended inconclusively, and early the following week Marcus brought the matter to the attention of the city's Bureau of Franchises, thereby opening up a controversy between the city and the utility which, at this writing three years later, has yet to be resolved.

Beginning with the intervention of Commissioner Marcus for reasons unrelated to the public weal, it became the position of the city that the rental being paid by Con Edison to run power lines above the aqueduct ought to be raised by an amount proportionate to the increase in the capacity of the lines. A self-congratulatory Con Edison report to its customers drew attention to the power increase: "Currently, we plan to replace an existing 138,000-volt line in Westchester with a 345,000-volt line that will carry nine times more power on the same right-of-way. This is the miracle of modern extra-high-voltage transmission. It is as though the automobile-carrying capacity of the Bronx River Parkway were increased nine times without widening it."

This report, written by Charles Luce himself and printed as an advertisement in New York and Westchester newspapers as a step in Con Edison's campaign to bolster an image which had been badly damaged by the 1965 power failure, stirred Itkin. "They didn't tell you they were going to increase it nine times?" he questioned Marcus.

The answer was no: "They said they would increase it a little bit."

Itkin was elated: "Here is your out. You can tell them

they didn't tell you the straight story, and you don't want to have any more meetings with anybody from Con Ed, that the lawyers can handle it and work out the franchise fee, and that you don't want to talk to anybody."

When city officials, alerted by Marcus, took the position that a ninefold increase in power justified a ninefold increase in rental, Chairman Luce characterized their logic as "ridiculous." He argued that the new line would take up less space than the existing line because it would be built on single steel poles instead of on the four-legged lattice-type towers then in use. Nevertheless, he was willing to accede to an increase in the city's compensation from $100,000 a year to as much as $200,000. Wherever justice resides in this dispute, it invites bemusement on the ways of government to consider that the matter might not have come up at all but for the tactics of Carmine De Sapio, the ingenuity of Herbert Itkin, and the desperation of James Marcus.

The water commissioner was being especially badgered during this time by former Consolidated Edison Chairman Charles Eble, who was not only a friend of Carmine De Sapio but was also close to New York County Republican Chairman Vincent Albano and his associate Joseph Ruggiero. It was at Albano's initiative that Marcus first met Eble and Vice-President Gerald Hadden at Toots Shor. Subsequently, Albano arranged for Marcus to meet with Eble again in the office of Deputy Mayor Robert Price. An ordinary businessman-commissioner get-together. Thereafter Eble, having gotten no satisfaction despite his good contacts, kept calling and kept being put off. The stall persisted until early in October when Itkin

171

notified Marcus that the hour had struck to make contact with the former head of the utility. Marcus was to call Eble at 11 a.m. on October 16 and make an appointment for the following day.

"The man made the call as he promised," Itkin reported to De Sapio—and the meeting was held, to no particular purpose. Marcus sums it up: "Mr. Eble said he knew I would do the right thing, and if there was anything he could do for me, to please let him know." The point of this exercise was to permit Carmine De Sapio or Henry Fried to call Eble *before* Marcus did and advise him that he would be hearing from the commissioner at the given hour of the given day—thereby putting on show their influence at the Municipal Building, and perhaps undercutting Vincent Albano.

In the following weeks there was action on all fronts. Negotiators for the city and the utility did their negotiating about a new price for the highline permit, to no avail. Itkin, or Mr. Herbert, kept in touch with Mr. Carl by telephone. (De Sapio denies ever using the name Mr. Carl. The closest he came to that, he says, was once when he allowed himself to be called Mr. Charles in a case of domestic delicacy involving friends of the family.) Itkin kept in constant touch with Marcus, exhorting him to Be Tough. Itkin, in turn, was being exhorted by Corallo. "Hey, make sure he makes that phone call," urged Tony Ducks a few days before the call to Eble, "because I don't know, with all the talk, I still don't know that guy, whether he is going to do what he promises or no." It was around Columbus Day and Marcus had gone off to his New Jersey house for the long weekend. "Stay on him, call him, get him," pressed Corallo. "He doesn't need vacations when we are all waiting for money." Several weeks later, still no scrap copper, still no money, Corallo made a scene in the Waldorf-Astoria's Peacock Alley. Itkin tells us that when he arrived for a meeting the racketeer introduced him to a companion with the words, "This is a great kid. I have been waiting for a year for my money, and I don't have it." He began pounding the table. "If you don't straighten this out within the month, I have had it with you and that commissioner and the rest of it. I am going directly to the people myself, and I'm telling you I am going to make the money. I have waited long enough for you characters. I got messed up on the first deal, it's not going to happen on this." He kept pounding the table, and the meeting broke up early.

Marcus's toughness or want of it comprised a great part of a conversation held in Itkin's apartment on October 11. Marcus and Corallo were visiting, and their host had taken the trouble to set up a tape recorder in his bedroom, the microphone hidden in a stereo speaker in the living room. It was at this meeting that Corallo first learned of De Sapio's entrance into the dealings with Con Edison. Itkin gave his version of Ulrich's maneuverings for position within the utility hierarchy. And Marcus, beset on all sides, told how tough he was being. He boasted that he had called one Con Edison vice-president a liar in front of his engineers. He boasted that he would order Luce "to stop sending his boys around." He boasted that he would tell the company's executives "to go fuck themselves."

There was precious little toughness in James Marcus's makeup. He had learned early that he could make his way better by adaptation than by resistance. By now, too, whatever self-esteem he may once have possessed had been broken by misfortune. He had become the total tool of plotters he scarcely knew in plots he took no part in devising. So, under the cold eye of Tony Ducks, he descended to the role of street-corner braggart. "Piss on Luce," said Commissioner Marcus.

The real James Marcus, whoever that was, rarely stood up. In his dealing with Con Edison, his shield was not toughness but vagueness. At a meeting in his office on November 1, 1967, with Chairman Luce and his vice-president for engineering, Marcus did not even call in a city engineer. Luce was baffled: "We'd gone down there specifically to talk about engineers' reports, and there were no engineers in sight." Marcus produced a report from a geologist which the Con Edison officials had already seen. He referred to another report on possible dangers to the aqueduct—but that one he didn't have with him. He wandered dolefully about the office and soliloquized upon his father's death and upon some problems related to the old Brooklyn Navy Yard. It was understandable that Luce should carry away from this meeting the sense that "we are getting a run-around from Mr. Marcus."

Twice, at the urging of Con Edison officials, Marcus had had typed the letter of permission on the highline, and twice, under the remonstrances of Itkin, he had held back from sending it. We may be sure that, put to the test, he would have had the letter typed a third time and would again have deposited it in his desk drawer. All unresisting now, he placed himself in the hands of fate—or, rather, left his fate in the hands of Itkin, Fried, De Sapio, and whoever else might show any interest in it. Every vestige of independence was gone, for independence could not save him now. He was prepared, if the heat generated by the utility became too uncomfortable, to give the permission it sought. From this extremity he appears to have been saved by Con Edison's own public-relations department, which, by advertising the expected ninefold increase in power, gave the city a bargaining issue that would serve for negotiation long after it could be of any use to James Marcus. So, in accord with De Sapio's program as well as with his own inclinations, Marcus devoted himself through the autumn weeks to avoiding conversation or contact with the utility's officials.

Early in November, Henry Fried learned from his man Hadden that the strategy was having its effect. At staff meetings, reported Hadden, the utility's engineers were complaining that "they were getting no place with the city people."

Upon this cue, Henry Fried told Hadden, "Maybe I can be of some help."

Until now, Carmine De Sapio had remained offstage. He had counseled the impresario Fried, had presumably chatted with Con Edison's Eble, and had devised scenes, through Itkin, for Marcus—but so far he had not put himself, his physical presence, his *reputation*, fully into play. The officials at Con Edison knew now that they were being given a run-around, but if Chairman Luce may be credited, he did not grasp the meaning of the commissioner's charade. It was time for this meaning to be made known—but making it known called for a certain tact. The new chairman of Con Edison, after all, was not Danny Motto. Luce could only be approached indirectly, through Hadden, or through Eble, or through Ulrich. It was time that he and his associates were given an inkling of whom they would have to deal with, if they hoped to deal with Commissioner Marcus. Not Milton Lipkins now, and not Vince Albano, but Carmine De Sapio.

On November 10, Sydney Baron, intimate of De Sapio and public-relations consultant to Con Edison at an annual retainer of $30,000, called Max Ulrich to a lunch at L'Aiglon.* Ulrich had encountered De Sapio before, at those quasi-public dinners, political *cum* charitable events, which politicians and businessmen use to advance their acquaintanceships and explore their mutual interests, but until now he had never had the pleasure of a lunch with the famous man. Baron opened the conversation with a put-down of Milton Lipkins: "Now, I know Lipkins well. He used to work for me, and I know his capabilities and I know his limitations, and I know a lot of Lipkins's talk." In contrast to the limited Lipkins stood Carmine De Sapio, whose knowledge of and experience in governmental affairs all the world acknowledged. Baron suggested that "Mr. De Sapio might be of some assistance to the company."

De Sapio followed this introduction by telling Ulrich of his reverence for Consolidated Edison and the Department of Water Supply—"two vital organizations in supplying the life blood of the city"—and of his concern over reports that had reached him to the effect that relations between the two vital organizations were not good. He then suggested, recalls Ulrich, that, given his own experience in government, he might be of some assistance

---

* The quality of restaurant frequented in the Consolidated Edison case shows a definite improvement over the Jerome Park reservoir case. Craig Claiborne gives L'Aiglon two stars. The Baroque, where Max Ulrich met with Sydney Baron and Milton Lipkins, gets three stars—"the menu is excellent and the service well above par."

to the utility—might, perhaps, be able to act "as some sort of referee."

De Sapio denies putting himself forward for his role: "I wasn't going to be offering my services as a referee in the Lindsay administration in the present position that I was in politically, which was negative." The Ulrich lunch, by his account, came about through an accidental meeting with Baron. He swears that he merely listened while Ulrich sang the Water Department blues, and his only suggestion was that Chairman Luce might take up the matter directly with the mayor. If that didn't work, De Sapio recalls himself as saying, with monumental propriety, "the only remedy I could suggest under the circumstances, on which I have had some experience in the past, was that they could initiate some kind of a lawsuit, if their aims were meritorious, against the Corporation Counsel, in order to remedy their wrongs."

Vice-presidents for public relations do not as a rule carry much weight within their company hierarchies—but Fried and De Sapio assumed that Ulrich would find it to his own advantage to bear to Irving Place the news that Carmine De Sapio was showing an interest in the riddle of James Marcus: Oedipus girding himself to confront the Sphinx. And so it turned out. Ulrich understood De Sapio's offer of assistance to the company to be "a matter of significance," and on his return to his office he discussed it not with the lately arrived Charles Luce but with his old boss, the friend of Albano and De Sapio, the veteran Eble.

A week later Fried let Hadden in on the news that he, Fried, had "someone" who might be of assistance in breaking through the Water Department's clogged pipes. That was on a Friday. On the following Monday, November 20,

Fried summoned Hadden to lunch at Tony's Wife, a restaurant on east Fifty-fifth Street.* There they were joined by Carmine De Sapio.

De Sapio's version of this meeting has him dropping into Tony's Wife in search of his employer and coming, by chance, upon Henry Fried, who introduced him to Gerald Hadden. He says he declined Fried's invitation to join them: "And I just went ahead and went back to the office and did some work." According to Hadden, the whole purpose of the November 20 lunch was to bring together Carmine De Sapio and himself.

Hadden's account fits snugly with Itkin's. That very day, Itkin tells us, De Sapio called him to say it was all right "to send that insurance policy out."

"Great!" cheered Itkin, and the next day, at the office of Marcus's attorney, where the commissioner was sorting through the depressing accounts of his finances, Itkin remarked to him, "Why don't you send that letter to my niece Plumps in England?"

"Okay," said Marcus—but it was after 5 p.m. when he got back to his office, and so he decided to put off until tomorrow what he had been instructed to do today.

On that tomorrow, the Wednesday before Thanksgiving, Hadden, Fried, and De Sapio met again at Tony's Wife. ("It never happened," declares De Sapio.) Here, according to Hadden, De Sapio asked whether Con Edison would be satisfied with a letter from the Water Department on the highline, instead of a more official document. "It would depend on what was said in the letter," replied

* "Tony's Wife is a New York institution with a host of devoted patrons, and the enthusiasm is not misplaced."—Craig Claiborne. Two stars. As Antonio Corallo's attorney took care to point out to his jury, the lady for whom the establishment is named bears no relation to his client.

Hadden. "If the letter was a granting of a permit, that would be it."

As the party broke up, De Sapio said to Hadden, "Well, I will see what I can do."

Having thus committed himself to produce a letter from Marcus—a commitment given, we may presume, in the understanding that Hadden would relay it to his superiors, just as Ulrich had—De Sapio was put out to find as the afternoon waned that the letter had still not been received. He complained to Itkin: "Well, I waited until the last mail, and I don't understand you, Herb. I thought everything was arranged, and I thought I made myself clear. They have not got the letter up at Con Ed. . . . I don't like to be made a fool of like this. Now, I am fulfilling what I said, and I certainly expect you fellows to do what I have just promised Con Ed I would do."

Itkin was suitably apologetic and at once called Marcus, whom he found in a jocular pre-holiday mood. Marcus chided his friend for uttering the name of De Sapio on the phone and for referring to the letter without the cover of "my niece Plumps in England." But he agreed to give the letter to his chauffeur to be hand-carried to Con Edison before 5 p.m.

That evening Itkin went to De Sapio's office, "expecting money," as he announced. De Sapio called Fried to okay payment: "Henry, I want to tell you that everything was done right."

Fried, in usual form, balked. The letter, he said, had been delivered to the wrong party at Con Edison. It had gone directly to Luce instead of to the executive—presumably Eble—who had been primed for it. "Just hold them off," Fried told De Sapio.

To which Carmine De Sapio responded with a sentence that adds luster to his dearly won reputation. "No," he said, "when I sell an insurance policy and it's purchased, then I have to see that the money is paid."

THIRTEEN

The $7,500 Misunderstanding

*"I don't think
that's fair, Carmine, I really don't."*
HERBERT ITKIN

COMMISSIONER Marcus's letter on the highline, first drafted in September and finally sent to Consolidated Edison in November upon Carmine De Sapio's okay and Herbert Itkin's signal, had been improved upon in accordance with the conspirators' strategy to delay the granting of permission. So cleverly had it been revised that in its final form, as Gerald Hadden told Henry Fried, it was "worthless" to the utility, hence not worth $25,000 to the businessman.

Permission was, "in principle," granted: "We have no objection to the principle of the proposed work as delineated in the brochure which you submitted to us, subject to approval by this department as to the design, specifications and method of constructing your proposed towers, including detailed designs and drawings of the proposed foundation and the proposed buried cable."

But the permission was no sooner offered than withdrawn. Chairman Luce needed a written statement strong enough to enable Con Edison to begin letting millions of dollars in contracts. What he got was this: "Moreover, it is understood that your company will not incur any expense in reliance on this approval in principle until such time as the Department notifies you in writing that it is satisfied that the contemplated construction will not cause harm to or in any way endanger the Catskill aqueduct referred to above."

And if this teasing treatment were not enough, the letter as finally sent contained still another sentence that put Con Edison farther back than the place where it had started in 1966: "It should be noted further that the present contract, dated May 15, 1959, granting permission for your present transmission system along the Catskill aqueduct right-of-way will have to be renegotiated with the Board of Estimate of the City of New York to provide for your contemplated construction." The city, remember, was asking for a ninefold increase in its rental, to match the advertised ninefold increase in power. "I couldn't believe that letter," says Luce.

Henry Fried, though willing enough to pay out cash in prospect of a decent return, was not a man to throw money away, particularly in the direction of a Herbert Itkin. Having obtained a Xerox copy of the letter, courtesy of Gerald Hadden, Fried balked at making his payoff for so unsatisfactory a piece of work. Why, after all, should he pay when Con Edison was unlikely to pay him back with contracts for this permission that was not a permission? He seemed not to appreciate that it was in the service of his own plot that the letter had become unsatisfactory. Nor did Carmine De Sapio. "There has been some talk that this is a very weak letter," De Sapio, in pajamas and robe, told Itkin, who had come expectantly to his apartment on lower Fifth Avenue on the Friday after Thanksgiving. Yet he handed over $5,000 in cash, presumably laid out in anticipation of reimbursement from Henry Fried.

De Sapio denies that he ever gave Itkin any money at any time, and there is no compelling evidence that he did, if one is not compelled by Itkin's testimony. Marcus, returned from his Thanksgiving weekend at the Jersey shore, asked Itkin about the promised $10,000. Itkin made no mention of the $5,000 already in his pocket, but emphasized instead Con Edison's dissatisfaction: "You may have to give them outright approval."

Marcus, broken and trained, unhesitatingly said that he would—though *how* he would, with negotiations on the rental under way, remains his secret; his bent was to agree today and leave tomorrow's problems for tomorrow.

That week, to continue with Itkin's account, he went to De Sapio's office in anticipation of the balance of the payoff. De Sapio gave him only $2,500, with the explanation that it would now be necessary to find out exactly what Con Edison wanted put into the letter so that it could be redone to specifications.

To which Itkin says he replied: "Look, Carmine, he sent the letter. We can't get around it. Now, I would like the rest of the money, really. We are expecting it, and you know the pressure that's on him right now."

"I understand there's pressure," conceded De Sapio, "but let's just see and make sure everything goes right. I have to get it all back from Henry Fried before I pay any more out."

On Monday, December 5, Itkin visited Carmine De Sapio for the last time. Their conversation, he reports, went as follows:

DE SAPIO: "You know, Herbert, this was a terrible letter,

183

and Henry decided that we are only going to get twenty thousand for the letter."

ITKIN: "All right, then we ought to take five thousand each and still give Marcus his ten."

DE SAPIO: "No, I think I have done an awful lot of work, and I think a lot of this has to do with Marcus not producing the proper letter, and I think that I am entitled to keep the seventy-five hundred I have gotten from Henry Fried. So you are only going to get five thousand more."

ITKIN: "I don't think that's fair, Carmine, I really don't."

DE SAPIO: "I do. You know, there is a lot more to go into. This is only the beginning with us, and I think Marcus has not been completely on the level because the letter is very weak, and he must know that the letter he is giving me and giving to us is weak, and they have been complaining to Henry Fried that it really says nothing."

De Sapio told Itkin to "be grown up about it" and began to count out the $5,000, putting onto the table two bundles of $2,000 each, in wrappers which Itkin noticed had an identifying mark. F.B.I.-man Itkin reports that he quickly swept them up, saying, "All right, Carmine, give me a thousand more." Evidently pleased that there was to be no further argument over the reduced payment, De Sapio counted out another thousand dollars from a roll of bills, and Itkin left "very rapidly."

The two wrappers, which Itkin subsequently turned over to his F.B.I. contact, emptied of cash ("I think, knowing me, they knew it must have been spent by that time"), were traced to a millionaire Queens builder and real-estate owner who sometimes placed large bets on horses with Henry Fried. In one such wager, in the fall of 1967, the builder lost about $4,000. He withdrew that sum from the Bank of North America, in two packets of $2,000, each within a paper wrapper. These he delivered to Henry Fried—and it was these wrappers that found their way to Herbert Itkin and in time to a federal courtroom.

Itkin apart, as we have noted, there is no evidence to connect De Sapio directly with the wrappers or with the passing of any money. At the very least, however, he appears to have been privy to Fried's designs. On December 5, Gerald Hadden tells us, he was again invited by Fried for lunch at Tony's Wife. (This restaurant was located conveniently neither for Fried nor for Hadden; but it was just across the street from De Sapio's office.) Hadden couldn't make it, but agreed to drop by at 2 p.m., at the conclusion of his own lunch date.* Fried was waiting for him, and they were joined by De Sapio. Hadden again expatiated upon the worthlessness of the highline letter.

There was a silence, broken by De Sapio. "Well," he said, "these people are hungry for money."

"How much?" asked Fried. "I'll give them forty thousand dollars."

Gerald Hadden could not have been shocked by the notion of a payoff. Even if he had failed to get the drift of Fried's intentions on his own, he had been told by Max Ulrich in an encounter in the hallway of their building that, on the basis of his lunch with Carmine De Sapio, Ulrich understood that the highline permit could be bought. Yet now Hadden, in the role of protector of Henry Fried's capital, says he showed indignation. "What are you paying anybody anything for?" he recalls himself as demanding. "Nothing has been done here. This is not a permit, this letter. No one has done anything." It was Hadden's way of

* At the Chateaubriand—one star.

telling Fried that no contracts could be expected for so hedged a document.

De Sapio played the conciliator: "Well, maybe they are entitled to a token of good faith." And Fried, over the objections of Hadden, said he would pay "them" $20,000.

If Itkin can be believed, the $20,000 had already been paid by the time of this odd conversation. If so, then the Fried-De Sapio duet had been rehearsed and staged for the benefit of Vice-President Hadden and, through him, the powers that had to be mollified at Consolidated Edison.

Exactly who was saying what to whom about the highline at the utility's offices on Irving Place during this period remains obscure. Marcus, having entrusted himself to Itkin or Fried or De Sapio or the Consolidated Edison Company, leaves no doubt that he was prepared to rewrite his letter to any and all specifications. As Itkin described his friend to an interested De Sapio: "Marcus is a man who twists one way or the other, and whoever is pushing him, he gives in." It is also clear that couriers were available to carry news from the cabal to Irving Place and back. What happened within the executive suite, however, is shrouded in discretion. Ulrich presents himself as a model of the proper vice-president. Hadden, testifying under a grant of immunity, could scarcely avoid incriminating himself, yet managed to keep an eye to his reputation.

The generals of the conspiracy, compelled to pitch their tents out of sight and sound of the field of action and to rely on couriers of mixed loyalties, could not be sure at any given moment how their campaign was progressing, if indeed it was progressing at all. Henry Fried was attuned to vibrations from Irving Place, but even his sensitive lis-

tening apparatus had been baffled by the major change in
Con Edison's management just as the highline campaign
was getting under way—the appointment on August 1,
1967, of Charles F. Luce to replace Charles E. Eble as
chairman of the board of Con Edison and its chief executive officer. Having an old friend give way to a complete
stranger at such a time was at best disconcerting. What
must have made the change downright worrisome for
Fried and De Sapio were the very different credentials of
the old chairman and the new one. Charles Eble was born
in New York in 1900. He was fifteen when he went to work
for the utility, then called Consolidated Gas, as a messenger at six dollars a week, and he stayed for the next fifty-
three years, ascending via the accounting department.
"How did he ever get to be head of Con Edison?" a young
Lindsay aide wondered on first meeting "the little fat
guy." Eble was active in many of the city's voluntary organizations, was well acquainted with politicians and
businessmen relevant to his company's concerns, and despite his modest formal schooling he was amply educated
in how matters were managed in New York. On taking
over the utility's chairmanship, he told a writer for *Fortune:* "Over the years I struck up friendships with many
politicians. It was not something that I set out to do objec-
tively at the beginning. But, as time passed, I found that
many of my friends had moved into positions of authority
in government. I could talk to them. It was as simple as
that."

Charles Luce had no equivalent experience of New
York's ways; his connections with authority lay elsewhere.
Born in Wisconsin, a gifted enough law student to become
clerk to Justice Hugo Black, he made his career in the

Northwest, specializing in power projects, with some Democratic politics on the side. In 1961 he was appointed Bonneville Power Administrator, and in 1966 he was named Under-Secretary of the Interior by President Johnson. It was from this office that he moved to Irving Place, bringing with him broad experience on a level of which Charlie Eble was innocent, prestige of a sort unusual for the utility's management, and no ties to New York's hovering politicos. He believed when he came to his post that "the day was past when Con Edison could sit down in the clubhouse and reach decisions. Now power is diffuse, all over town. It's no longer possible to deal with two or three people."

Luce assesses Max Ulrich's failure to report to him the overtures of Lipkins as "an error of judgment." But the judgment was sound enough. Luce had no experience in big-city dealing. He had never met Carmine De Sapio or Henry Fried, and he decided early to sever his company's arrangement with Sydney Baron, over the protests of Ulrich and other executives: "They told me, 'He has a big ear'—that he knew things that Con Ed ought to know. But I couldn't find that Baron did thirty thousand dollars' worth of anything for us." Not the sort of boss to whom one would feel comfortable trying to explain the propositions of Milton Lipkins or Carmine De Sapio. Instead, Ulrich reported to the experienced Charles Eble, who relayed nothing of the matter to Luce. Later Eble would explain that he didn't think the suggestion of a payoff to Marcus was genuine, and, anyway, he felt that the new chairman had enough on his mind. The coming of Charles Luce, then, can only have been a snag in the Fried-De Sapio strategy. Charles Eble finally retired from Con Edison as planned in June 1968, coincident with the reservoir trial.

Whatever the jostling within Con Edison, Henry Fried was not destined to add tens of millions of dollars in utility contracts to the millions he already had. The treasure of scrap metal that gleamed in Antonio Corallo's head was to be snuffed out. And James Marcus, having made his last grab at salvation, was to come away empty-handed. Itkin claims that he shared with his partner the cash he obtained from De Sapio, but Marcus denies receiving a penny of it. He called Itkin on the afternoon of December 5: "We agreed to send the letter. We sent the letter. We need the money. How come the money hasn't been paid?" Itkin laid the blame on De Sapio, who, he said, was refusing to complete the payoff because he had learned that Marcus was under investigation by the district attorney. In order to accept Marcus's testimony over Itkin's on this point, we need only allow that Itkin was capable, in these final faltering days of their partnership, of grabbing whatever he could for himself.

It was on the evening of December 5, says Itkin, that Marcus came to him for $1,000 in pocket money so that he might entertain some friends at a theater benefit that evening: "This is my last shot and I want to do it right." (The event in question was a revival of George Kelly's comedy, *The Show-Off*.) Itkin says he handed over the $1,000; Marcus denies asking for it or getting it. Whichever of them one chooses to believe, the day was a special one for James Marcus. A few hours before curtain time, he had had to perform in a New York grand-jury room. A week later he sent to the mayor his resignation as Commissioner of the Department of Water Supply, Gas and Electricity.

Denouement

"You're in a lot of trouble."
HERBERT ITKIN *to James Marcus,*
September 1967

IN December 1965, Conestoga, Ltd., served as a curtain-raiser for James Marcus's brief performance as a dishonest public official. In September 1967, Conestoga returned from the wings and the curtain began to descend. The Conestoga partner based in Europe, Peter Littman, had complained to the New York District Attorney's office about the manner in which his associates in Manhattan were using $16,000 that he had handed over for investment in Xtra. The complaint drew the district attorney's attention to Commissioner Marcus, and so began the process which would end with his resignation, his conviction on an altogether different charge brought by a different prosecutor, and his imprisonment.

Conestoga had, in fact, lain idle for months, since the fall of 1966, when the partnership between Marcus-Itkin on one side and Greenfield-Littman on the other was dissolved. The reason for the dissolution, according to Itkin, was that Marcus refused to play his appointed part as front man. A meeting would be arranged, for example, in Switzerland, with *"several very big Nigerians,"* and Conestoga's front man would not show up—or, if he did, it was

only to bemoan his own predicament with Xtra. Marcus
has a different explanation. He attributes the breakup to
Albert Greenfield's offer of a five-percent kickback to Marcus-Itkin for any city contracts that might be awarded to a
firm in which Greenfield had a substantial interest.

Greenfield grants that he was not oblivious to the opportunities that a relationship with a high New York City
official might open to him—"Part of being in business is to
plumb your connections"—but denies that he reached the
point of discussing payoff percentages with Marcus. Even
if he had, it is not easy to understand wherein the suggestion of a bribe should have offended the Marcus-Itkin
sensibility. We need look no further for the cause of
dissatisfaction on the part of Greenfield than to his dis-
covery that Marcus-Itkin were using the company (and
his name) for their own unorthodox activities. Though the
company was never incorporated, showed no profits, and
did nothing that could strictly be called business, Marcus-
Itkin managed to collect some thousands of dollars as
"retainers" for unconsummated deals.

In the summer of 1967, Peter Littman demanded back
the money he had entrusted to Marcus for the purchase of
shares in Xtra. He had never received any confirmation
that his investment had in fact been invested, and his erstwhile partners had been giving only evasive answers to his
months of inquiries on the subject. Itkin concedes that
the partners did not have the cash to repay Littman, but
he adds, "We could've vigged it like we did before." Up
until this time, maintains Itkin, he had no notion that
Marcus was unable to cover all the losses he had suffered
on Xtra; he assumed it was only a question of selling a few
other securities. Itkin professes to have been astonished to

learn from Peter Littman that the latter's check, instead of being used to purchase stock, had been endorsed by Marcus and deposited to the account of his wife Lily. "Marcus lived such a complete lie that none of us knew how bad off he was," says Itkin—and he adds, without humorous intent, "If you lie enough, you begin to live your lie."

Finally, Littman, urged on by his irate brother-in-law Greenfield, went to the district attorney—"a matter of principle," says Itkin. It seems to have worked in practice, for a few weeks later, according to Marcus, the complaining partner was repaid with interest. But the interest of the district attorney had meanwhile been awakened.

It is tempting at this point to linger over a nice irony—that the public criminal Marcus should have been brought down by a private delinquency of a few thousand dollars, and that if not for this thing he might have lived out his career in honor and prosperity, collecting kickbacks from the city's contractors as long as John Lindsay held office, and then perhaps joining the train of that estimable public servant to Albany or to Washington or wherever destiny and duty called. Yet even if Littman had been pacified, we may be certain that Marcus would, in a short time, have been traded off by his partner Itkin. Not that Itkin had such a denouement clear in his mind all along. Not at all. His reports to the F.B.I., which began in 1963, dealt solely with peculiarities in the investment of Teamster pension funds. He told his contact, Special Agent William Vericker, nothing about the reservoir bribe until the summer of 1967, when it was all over.*

* Although Vericker received his first inkling of Marcus's involvement in August 1967, it was not until his indictment in December that Mayor Lindsay learned the cheerless details of the case. In explanation of this want of courtesy on the part of the F.B.I., *New York Times* Associate Edi-

By then Itkin, to his distress, confusion, and indignation, had been charged by the New York district attorney
with grand larceny. This case began in the fall of 1964,
when one Bernard W. Robbins, owner of the Highway
House motel in Tucson, Arizona, gave Itkin $15,000 for
assistance in obtaining a $1.5 million mortgage on his
property, conventional lending institutions having proved
unresponsive. When months went by without action on
the mortgage and without return of his front money, Robbins put in a complaint with the district attorney's office.
Agent Vericker, coordinator of the F.B.I.'s "criminal informants program," learned of it, and in April 1966 he suggested that Itkin pay a call on the district attorney. There
an arrangement was made with Assistant District Attorney
Frank Rogers whereby the Robbins complaint would be
shelved on condition that Itkin produce information of use
to the D.A.'s office. For the next six or seven months Itkin
served as an informer for the district attorney. Four times
he had a miniature tape recorder strapped to his body and
went out to meet with suspect individuals. Despite such
exertions, in the fall of 1966, the arrangement was termi-

---

tor Tom Wicker quotes "a veteran government official with first-hand
knowledge of the F.B.I. and the ways of its director," who asked himself
"why Hoover didn't tip off Lindsay in time to spare him some embarrass-
ment or at least put him on guard. That's what you'd normally expect and,
in this case, Hoover would know that Lindsay might some day be President
and the F.B.I. would have to work with him. Then I remembered that
when Lindsay was a Justice Department lawyer for Herbert Brownell in
the fifties, he had to go into the Supreme Court and plead a case on appeal in which the principal witnesses were F.B.I. informants, and the
F.B.I. had refused to show the defendant their files substantiating the informants' testimony. They brought their justification to Lindsay, and he
looked at it and said something like, 'You guys must be kidding.' " There
may be less here than meets the suspicious eye. Whatever Hoover's pre-
dilections, he does not seem to be in the habit of leaking information on
ongoing investigations to interested politicians.

nated. Itkin attributes the breakup to his fear of a leak in the D.A.'s office. Given the choice of entering the service of the district attorney or being indicted, he says he chose a quiet indictment as a way of maintaining his cover, and the following April he was in fact indicted in the Robbins case. The event attracted no great notice. The trial was set for May but was repeatedly postponed as Itkin changed lawyers, until in March 1968 the district attorney again sought his assistance—this time in the De Sapio case. At this writing, Itkin has still not gone to trial on the Robbins charge, owing to the benign intercession of the federal prosecutor. (The district attorney's office declines to give its version of this Itkin interlude.)

Itkin's actions from the spring through the fall of 1967 —between his indictment and the exposure of Marcus— are not a model of clarity; they suggest the contradictory impulses that generated his bizarre career. First, as always, he wanted money—which, though in insufficient amounts, the partnership with Marcus was bringing him. (He estimates that $120,000 in payoffs was collected during their collaboration; there is no reason to assume the sum was divided equally. Says Itkin, "My primary motive was never to make the money.") While working out deals for Marcus-Itkin, he needed to maintain his standing with the F.B.I.; there lay his hope of escaping prosecution for a multitude of offenses. "I was perhaps reckless," he conceded after his exposure as both criminal and informer, when he had settled upon his line of defense and perhaps his deeper rationalization, "but I did whatever I did for good motives. I was hoping to obtain evidence for the United States government." In his cluttered imagination,

Itkin may have seen himself as carrying off a remarkable coup—keeping his relationship with Marcus intact while serving up diverse Mafiosi and Teamster officials and go-betweens to J. Edgar Hoover. It was a mad hope, and as conflicting pressures began to converge on him in the spring and summer of 1967—the indictment in New York, the Justice Department's need to bring the pension-fund cases to court within the statute of limitations, the prospect of a windfall from Consolidated Edison—he was like the clown-juggler who keeps tossing more and more objects into the air until the big hilarious moment when they fall crashing to the ground on all sides of him.

Within the bustle of Itkin's final pre-exposure months, we can spy the glimmerings of his scheme. While continuing to lay hands on as much cash as he could, he sought to ingratiate himself with the F.B.I., looking toward the day when he would have to depend on the Justice Department for immunity from prosecution. The special difficulty, as Itkin had become "acutely aware," was that the F.B.I. was required, by its own internal regulations, "to disseminate to local prosecutive agencies any information brought to its attention where federal jurisdiction does not apply." It was a most disturbing requirement, since it would have subjected Itkin to further harassment from the district attorney. Arguing that such dissemination might interfere with federal cases then being pursued, he prevailed on the F.B.I. to hold off on its disseminating process for a while at least.

Beginning in the spring of 1967, after his indictment, Itkin did what he could to bolster his standing as a federal informant. His most adventurous effort—one that must have appealed to his self-image as the undercover operative nonpareil—was to plaster a recording device into the walls of his apartment for the purpose of capturing the utterances of guests like Antonio Corallo. He told his F.B.I. contact of this plan in May and was given the official position of the Bureau. Agent Vericker reports: "We told him that if he did this it was purely of his own volition; he was on his own." Which Itkin sensibly took to mean that the Bureau would be delighted to have a chance at any recordings that happened to come its way through the spontaneous efforts of a conscientious citizen. Given this much encouragement, he assigned Charles Rappaport to seek out information about recording devices from a friend and client who was in the business. A few weeks later Rappaport's friend appeared at their office, and Itkin explained that he wanted a reliable machine that could be left unattended and would pick up voices at a distance of twenty or thirty feet without interference from an air conditioner.

"At this time," says the audio man, "I got a little upset, wondering what the machine was going to be used for." He expressed concern about Itkin's desire for a concealed microphone, whose use might compromise the supplier as well as the supplied.

Itkin assured him that everything was "perfectly open and aboveboard."

Then why hide the machine? The salesman reports: ". . . at that point he [Itkin] said, being a client of Mr. Rappaport and because of my close personal relationship with Mr. Rappaport, he would state to me that he and Mr. Rappaport were doing something for the F.B.I., the nature of which he did not want to discuss with me—and I was just as happy not to learn about it since it was none of my business to begin with."

When Rappaport confirmed Itkin's claim, the machine was supplied. Rappaport's confirmation cannot be taken as proof that he altogether comprehended or credited Itkin's connection with the F.B.I.; by now he was simply accustomed to following Itkin along whatever routes, into whatever back alleys the latter chose to move. The recording device was installed in July,* and Itkin turned over to the F.B.I. several not entirely audible tapes featuring Antonio Corallo. It was from one such tape that the F.B.I. first learned, in August, that Consolidated Edison was on the conspirators' minds, and first heard, in October, the name of Carmine De Sapio used in connection with that conspiracy.

Itkin's design to keep the case within the federal ambiance, where he felt some security about his future, was jeopardized in November 1967 when Charles Rappaport turned over their joint checkbook to the district attorney. It was Rappaport's fortune that the investigation into Marcus's affairs began when it did. There is no doubt that he was implicated in crooked activities and had been at least since joining Itkin (who charges that Rappaport helped himself to $35,000 from their checking account)— but he had not yet had a chance to advance much beyond

---

* When technical difficulties developed at the end of July, the device had to be returned to Rappaport's friend, who was surprised to find the microphone missing. He called Itkin, who "explained to me the microphone was totally inaccessible. I said it is a small little microphone, that he could carry it in a lunch bag or could fit it into his pocket. He explained it was plastered in the wall of his apartment. . . ."

messenger boy for the principal conspirators. That saving innocence or ineptitude, recognized by a jury, would bring him acquittal in the 1968 trial. Given another year or two of instruction by Itkin, the young lawyer might, with diligence, have worked his way up to full complicity and fallen with the rest.

Rappaport seems to have been lucky, too, in his choice of an attorney who evidently advised him in November to hand over the checkbook to the district attorney, at a time when Itkin was doing his best to scare him into leaving town, with tales of the vengeance of Tony Ducks. Itkin claims that Corallo showed irritation with him for not keeping closer watch over his apprentice after that young man had been summoned by a grand jury: "How could you not know, from the time that he talks to the state grand jury to now, not know where he is? You must know! . . . You better find out, and if he keeps his mouth shut, we'll be all right. God knows what that kid is going to say." According to Itkin, Rappaport was hysterical after his first questioning by the district attorney: "I'm scared. . . . What am I going to do?" Itkin recalls himself as replying: "Charlie, I don't know yet, but you got to trust me. Now, go out of town, call me on Sunday, and I'll tell you what to do."

By this time Rappaport, though still under Itkin's guidance, evidently knew enough of his methods to become nervous when asked to trust him. The young man was scarcely a threat to Corallo, with whom he had had little direct dealing; but as possessor of the joint checkbook, he was singularly well informed about most of Itkin's ventures. At his first meetings with the district attorney's staff, Rappaport, in line with Itkin's directive, invoked an attorney-client privilege, the strategy being that as Itkin's attorney he could not be compelled to discuss his mentor's life and works. Early in December, Itkin sent Rappaport a carefully drawn letter which, under the pretext of permitting Rappaport to testify about Marcus's affairs, emphasized that he was bound to confidence regarding Itkin's affairs. It warrants reprinting here, both for its own spurious sake and because it makes clear what worried Itkin about the district attorney's investigation:

Dear Sir:

I hereby consent to your disclosing to the District Attorney of New York County or the grand jury of said county any and all details of any transaction of any kind whatsoever you may have conducted in my behalf in connection with the affairs of James L. Marcus, and I expressly waive any and all of my rights which do or may exist under the attorney and client relationship and release you from any and all liabilities in connection with such disclosures. This waiver and release is expressly limited to my relationship, personal, business or professional, with James L. Marcus.

Very truly yours,
Herbert Itkin

At the same time that Itkin was doing all he could to discourage Rappaport from cooperating with the district attorney, he was encouraging him to talk to the F.B.I. For a lawyer with a taste for "finder's fees," the terms were enticing: Itkin's finder's fee from the Justice Department was to be immunity from prosecution, and although Rappaport was no great prize, he would serve as a show of good faith. So in the middle of December Itkin gave a series of talks to his young man which make rather Pecksniffian reading. Itkin, who had taught Rappaport much of what he knew of the crooked world, now told him: "Charlie, for one time in your life, you are doing the right thing." Itkin said: "I believe they are bringing out one of the first real indictments against organized crime in the City of New York, which shows the corruption and everything else, and, Charlie, one of the things is you really don't have to worry too much because if they [the Mafia] are going to be after anybody, it will be me, because they considered me part of them. You really don't have to worry for either your wife or your kids, because I think if anybody is the one they are coming after, it will be me." Itkin said: "It takes a lot of guts to stand up to these guys. What we are doing is one of the greatest things, and you can be proud of it and your children can be proud of it." Itkin said: "You are doing a great thing, and whether we get indicted or not, this is one time, Charlie, that you can be proud of yourself as a man and you are really standing up. If there were enough people in this country who did it, we could once and for all destroy organized crime." Quoth Itkin: "A person like you in twenty cities of this country, coming forth like you are, in one fell swoop could really destroy what has existed for many, many years, and you ought to be very proud of yourself."

All of this, coming from one who had already taught Rappaport so much, must have been edifying, but Rappaport (and presumably the attorney he had by now consulted) had in mind a more useful form of appreciation from the federal government than Itkin's esteem. Rappaport wanted what Itkin would attain—immunity from prosecution in the federal courts. We may take it as certain that Itkin was not above leaving the impression with

Rappaport that the two of them would be indicted merely to maintain their "cover" for as long as possible.

Rappaport told what he knew to the F.B.I. agents. Then, on December 19, 1967, contrary to Itkin's advice, he told what he knew to the district attorney's men—and received immunity from prosecution on that front. So ended the marriage of Itkin and Rappaport. In the federal trial that followed, Rappaport was indicted—and not as a cover—and Itkin exerted himself in his testimony to bolster the government's weak case against the young man by bringing in his name on every possible occasion. It was not for want of trying by Itkin that Rappaport—who, in another courtroom, might have been the district attorney's key witness against Itkin—was acquitted. At the end, Itkin, like the eunuch Eutropius detested by Gibbon, came "to abhor the instrument of his own crimes." The district attorney's grant of immunity to the young man struck him as "rather shocking," and the kindest words he would thereafter find for his erstwhile protégé were "embezzler" and "male whore."

The end of Itkin's fading relationship with James Marcus was foreshadowed in September 1967 when the district attorney invited the commissioner in to discuss certain matters to which investigators had been drawn while following up the complaint of Conestoga partner Littman. Their interest was piqued in particular by a deposit of $55,000 which had been added to Marcus's account with Koenig & Co. in October 1966. When Marcus told Itkin of his visit to the district attorney—"They are asking me questions that I am going to find impossible to answer"— Itkin replied with one of those exquisite sentences that become classics at the moment they are uttered. Said Itkin to Marcus: "You're in a lot of trouble."

In the weeks that followed, Itkin became more helpful. Marcus attributes to him the inspiration for his explanation to the district attorney that the $55,000 had come from his father. (Itkin refuses credit for this limp tale. It was Marcus's brain child, he maintains—which, if so, makes it one of the few original ideas that Marcus seems to have come up with during their entire acquaintance. In December 1967, when Marcus, back to the wall now, was ready to go to the F.B.I.—"All I wanted to do was go there and tell my story"—Itkin was more than ready to go with him. They went together to the office at 201 East Sixty-ninth Street, where Itkin presented Marcus to Special Agent Vericker. Though Marcus insists that the decision was his alone, the fact that he chose to tell his story to the F.B.I. rather than to the district attorney (and, in fact, perjured himself before a New York County grand jury) bespeaks Itkin's influence. On the model of Baron Munchausen, who was able to leap from cannonball to flying cannonball, until he was carried safely back to his home camp, Itkin had managed to ride his criminal deals as long as possible, and when that became impossible, he jumped onto his deals with the law. James Marcus was the trophy that Herbert Itkin brought home from the jungle.*

* In the course of their relationship, Itkin had let drop an unprompted word or two about his connection with the F.B.I. Marcus's response to such hints was brought out under cross-examination at the 1968 trial:

COUNSEL: You knew he [Itkin] was an agent at that time [December 1967]. Is that correct?

MARCUS: I knew what he had told me. He told me a lot of things over a period of years.

COUNSEL: Did you believe him?

MARCUS: It did not matter really.

COUNSEL: I asked you a question, yes or no, did you believe him?

On December 14 Marcus told his story to a federal grand jury, and on December 18 the other principals in the reservoir payoff found themselves summoned to the federal courthouse for the same purpose. There, Itkin swears, Henry Fried counseled him, "They'll never get anything on us if we all shut up." As their turns came, Henry Fried and Daniel Motto went into the grand-jury room and denied any wrongdoing. (Carl D'Angelo, later to be named as a co-conspirator in the disappointed hope that he would cooperate with the prosecution, also appeared before the grand jury and denied all. He was Motto's attorney at the time and says that he advised his client "to tell the truth." Motto did not take that advice.) After hearing the testimony, the grand jury brought its indictments against Fried, Motto, Corallo, Rappaport, and Marcus.

By then James Marcus was a *former* water commissioner. On December 12, the day of his first visit to the F.B.I., he had drawn up a resignation requested by the mayor, who still did not appreciate the extent of his friend's malfeasance. In a letter which is of a piece with the rest of his career in municipal government, Marcus wrote:

> Within the last few weeks, a number of purely personal problems have arisen which have required considerable attention on my part. This, coming close upon the death of my father, together with other family problems, might seriously interfere with my

---

MARCUS: Occasionally I did and occasionally I did not.
COUNSEL: Did you believe him in connection with the statement that he was an agent for the F.B.I.?
MARCUS: I was not sure.
Marcus understood enough about Itkin not to seek to understand more.

effectiveness as commissioner. Therefore, and regrettably, I respectfully request to be relieved of my duties.

In complete fairness to you, I must advise you as to the nature of these matters. Before joining your administration, I was engaged in a business venture which became involved in numerous transactions. One of the persons with whom I dealt made a complaint to the District Attorney of New York County, which that agency is naturally inquiring into. Please be assured that the complaint has nothing whatever to do with my official duties and that I am, in fact, free of any wrongdoing.

Under all the circumstances, I believe it best that I submit my resignation. I do so with deepest regret. My work has been a satisfying and challenging experience, and my association with you and the other members of your administration thoroughly gratifying.

On the morning of December 13, 1967, Gerald Hadden learned from a radio newscast that Marcus had resigned. The implications were not lost upon him: "I was very much concerned. I was involved with this business of discussing a permit with the Marcus organization." So he called Henry Fried and they met for lunch at the Richelieu. There Hadden expressed his concern and was told, "Don't worry about him." Fried informed Hadden that he had paid out the $20,000 in the Con Edison matter, and then he handed his friend an envelope with $5,000 in it, as "a Christmas present."

Vice-President Hadden's supplemental income from Henry Fried—which he hastened to remove from his safe-deposit vault and put in a bureau drawer at home—was still a secret from his superiors, but the December 18 indictments in the reservoir case called their attention to Fried himself. The holidays passed, and on January 4 Chairman Luce reached a decision to remove Fried from the utility's bidding list. The contractor had strong defenders among the utility's senior executives; nonetheless, he would no longer be in the running for construction work from Con Edison that had been bringing his firms nearly $10 million a year. Luce also hired outside counsel to carry forward an investigation, on the reasoning, more apt than he knew, that "Anybody who will bribe a city official will bribe anybody who's for sale."

The utility's administrative vice-president, Donham Crawford, was given the job of breaking the news to Fried —a trying experience, as it turned out. Crawford called the contractor to his office on January 5 and delivered the judgment: "I told Mr. Fried that the company had decided to remove his name from the bidding list for future work." Fried grew impassioned. He reminded Crawford that his companies had served Con Edison satisfactorily for many years. He reminded him, too, that a defendant is innocent until proved guilty—yet here he was being thrown out on the street on the basis of newspaper publicity. He protested that he hardly knew the other persons mentioned in the stories. He asked that he be permitted, at least, to continue to bid on per diem contracts and on the ash-handling contracts.

Crawford, without latitude in the matter, could offer only the slim comfort that if Fried were able to clear his name, the decision would be reconsidered—but, for the time being, he was scratched: "I told him that that was the policy that the company had decided upon, and that that would be the way it was. He could not bid on any new work."

At this, Crawford relates, Fried said, "out of a clear blue sky": "Well, you know, twenty thousand dollars has been provided to Mr. Marcus." And he went on, somewhat incoherently, to tell of a luncheon he had had with people whose initials were J.H. and C.D. Crawford was at first impatient: "When he started using initials he became a little confusing, and I didn't want to get into a detailed discussion of this matter with Mr. Fried, because I didn't believe what he was saying." But gradually he got Fried's drift: "It seemed pretty clear to me that he was inferring that somebody in our company had to undertake such an alleged transaction." Crawford put the question to Fried: "Are you saying to me that someone in Edison Company asked you to provide twenty thousand dollars to Mr. Marcus to obtain approval on a transmission-line permit?"

"Yes, I am," declared Fried. "It was Gerry Hadden."

In his desperation, Fried produced Hadden's name like a credit reference that could somehow reinstate him with Con Edison. But Hadden's own credit was fast running out. The next day, a Saturday, he was summoned to Chairman Luce's home in Bronxville and told of Fried's charge. Hadden admitted that he had known of the proposed payoff to Marcus but denied having anything to do with it. He made no mention of Fried's monthly envelopes. It was a calm meeting, but it ended with Luce angry that Hadden had said nothing of what he knew during their conferences on removing Fried from the bidding list.

The following Monday, January 8, Hadden made a desperate attempt to save face, and perhaps job. As Fried had tried to use him, so now he tried to use Fried. He prevailed on the businessman to come to his office early that morning. Hadden could not deny having lunched with Fried and De Sapio and discussed the highline permit— and one might even interpret that meeting as having been in Con Edison's interests. But with Fried up for trial there could be no explaining away a connection with a $20,000 payoff. Having pointed out this difficulty to Fried, Hadden asked Crawford to step into his office. We have Crawford's account of the meeting: "I went in and Mr. Hadden was there and Mr. Fried was sitting by his desk. Mr. Hadden said that he had asked Mr. Fried to be there so that I could hear from Mr. Fried that he, Mr. Hadden, was not involved in the matter that Mr. Fried had said he was involved in the preceding Friday. Mr. Hadden turned to Mr. Fried and said 'Isn't that right, Henry?' Mr. Fried said, 'Yes, that's right.' "

At this dramatic point, Hadden was summoned to Luce's office, leaving Crawford alone with an agitated Fried. "Mr. Fried was considerably exercised, I thought— began to rave and rant." The gist of the ranting was that a full exposé was in the offing, that Carmine De Sapio was going to be subpoenaed, that Fried's records, including the guest list of his yacht, would be subpoenaed, and so forth.

Crawford blandly asked why that should concern Consolidated Edison, since Fried had just assured him that Hadden was not involved. Fried, still confident that the utility would have to come to the protection of its own, answered: "Well, I just said that so that you would not be aware that he was a participant, but the fact is he was a participant." He added that two other company officers, Max Ulrich and Thomas Duncan, knew something of the

207

deal, and that Carmine De Sapio "had to be made whole." Having delivered himself of this implicit threat to defame high executives of the utility, he asked to see Chairman Luce. Crawford left the office to relay Fried's latest disclosures to the chairman, and then reported back that Mr. Luce was not interested in talking to Mr. Fried. The contractor was invited to send in his complaints in writing.

During his Saturday conversation with Luce, Hadden, perhaps seeking companionship in misery, told his chief that he had learned from Max Ulrich that someone named Itkin had been trying to contact company executives about the highline. When Luce put this to Ulrich that afternoon, Ulrich replied that it was not *Itkin* but *Lipkins* who had suggested to him that approval for the right-of-way might be obtained if preference were shown to the contractor Orlando. This suggestion Ulrich had imparted to outgoing Chairman Eble. The contract that Orlando had lately obtained from Con Edison was immediately canceled and Vice-President Hadden was given his choice of resigning or retiring. As for Vice-President Ulrich, whether his transfer to Brooklyn is taken as promotion or exile depends on how one feels about Brooklyn.

The name "Itkin" hovered about these commotions on Irving Place, a presence influencing the fates of men who, up to that time, had scarcely an inkling of what sort of thing an Itkin might be.

After the prosecution rested its case in the Marcus-Co-rallo-Fried-Motto-Rappaport trial, defense counsel offered an array of motions for dismissal of the proceedings. In addition to the customary grounds, they complained that F.B.I. informer Itkin had in fact entrapped the other alleged conspirators. Although the thought of Tony Ducks having to be lured into a criminal act captured one's fancy, the motions were turned down by Judge Edward Weinfeld, who presided throughout in a most meticulous manner. Judge Weinfeld ruled:

> The fact of the matter is that the evidence is clear beyond any question in the Court's view that this was an independent venture of his [Itkin's] own; that he participated on his own, and was not initiated by the Government in any respect. That it was after the entire transaction was over that he informed the Government as to the nature of the transaction. I find no basis of any kind to the claim of entrapment. The evidence is clear on it. The fact that he informed with respect to other transactions during this particular transaction does not lead to the entrapment of anybody here.

Like surgeons operating on Siamese twins, the federal prosecutors had managed to sever Itkin from Marcus, saving the one in order to destroy the other.

The evidence did show what Judge Weinfeld said it showed—but that left Itkin in a strikingly ambiguous position: an informer who did not always inform; a conspirator in crime with attachments to the F.B.I. The Bureau denies that their informant #3936C was "directed" to go out and get information in the Consolidated Edison case or any case. As Agent Vericker, the agency's specialist on informers, sketches the relationship: "There were times during the course of these five years when he had indicated he had met or had some business dealings with people, and he would ask if we were interested in this particular party, and I would say yes, if the party was a labor racketeer, a political figure, a member of the organized-crime group." Had Vericker conceded a more intimate relationship, Itkin's status as a witness for the prosecution would have been compromised. Itkin assesses himself: "I had to walk a tightrope. You can't be all white. You have to be sort of a gray character."

As saintly sinner, or sinning saint, Herbert Itkin became a source of conflict between U.S. Attorney Robert M. Morgenthau, who needed his testimony in several cases of consequence, and Manhattan District Attorney Frank Hogan, who was bent on bringing him to trial. Hogan's insistence on fighting the U.S. Attorney over Itkin is puzzling, unless one lays it to simple pique over having had a juicy case snatched away from him. Itkin naturally suggests that Hogan was motivated by his friendly feelings for Carmine De Sapio, dating from the time when the political boss tried to turn the district attorney into a senator. The D.A.'s efforts to get hold of him on indictments in the Marcus case, Itkin marks down as "a very destructive thing. It will hurt informants and ruin stool pigeons. . . . It can't help law enforcement." (Around the D.A.'s office he is reportedly known as "the germ.")

In the course of this dispute, Morgenthau's office asked the C.I.A. for a statement that national-security considerations precluded the prosecution of former agent Herbert Itkin. This the C.I.A. could not bring itself to provide—either because it would have been untrue or because such a public concession that the C.I.A. has something to do with national security would amount to a violation of agency policy. But the C.I.A. did come through with an ambiguously worded affidavit to the effect that Itkin had been its

unpaid informant "since prior to 1964." Officials explain
privately that the affidavit was the agency's way of assist-
ing the federal prosecutor without telling a falsehood.

Itkin was indicted by a New York County grand jury in
June 1968 for his part in the bribing of James Marcus by
the Vintray operators and for conspiring with Marcus to
commit perjury. His lawyer—who is presumably paid by
the government, since Itkin admits to having no money—
brought proceedings to transfer the indictments to the
federal jurisdiction on the grounds that Itkin had been
"acting as an informer for the Federal Bureau of Investigation." And so he appears to have slipped from the grasp
of the state. (Should Itkin yet find himself a defendant in
state court, a reporter for the *Village Voice* has pointed
out, his trial may well be presided over by a judge with
debts to Carmine De Sapio.) Whatever the destiny of Itkin's soul, his body remains under close guard at a military
base near New York City.

Even after going into protective custody in January
1968, Itkin played on the ambiguity of his role. He would
maintain at the Marcus trial later that year that he had
considered himself "a part of organized crime," and in
February he threatened to cease informing and revert to
his authentic profession. He told a C.I.A. contact, perhaps
the one who had brought him to the F.B.I. in 1963: "I
have made all arrangements to pull out of this place and
turn back to the boys. I'm pulling out and I am going to
make a real stink about this whole F.B.I. deal. How I enticed and entrapped not only Marcus and Rappaport, but
how I enticed several of the others." Itkin explains this
threat as an effort to compel the federal authorities to
place under protection the children of his second wife,

who had been removed from their mother's custody in 1966* and were then living with their father in Peekskill, New York: "I was trying to protect two little boys who I am dreadfully afraid will be killed." Itkin says that during his days with the mob he was in on many conversations where the families of potential witnesses were threatened, and he claims that he pleaded with his federal guardians: "Let me out in the street, and at least the people will come after me and not the kids."

In their cross-examination, defense attorneys affected hearty skepticism of his explanation—though they could not always agree on whether the man was a full-blooded F.B.I. agent who had entrapped their clients or a thoroughgoing scoundrel whose testimony was unworthy of credit. Noting that he had tried to prevail upon the Justice Department to bring criminal charges against his wife's former husband—which, in his own words to a member of the U.S. Attorney's office, "would cinch the granting of custody of the children to their mother"—and had actually gotten an assistant U.S. attorney to testify in his behalf at a custody hearing in Westchester Family Court, the defense tried to leave the impression that Itkin was

---

* Itkin and his wife protest that the father regained custody of the children on a technicality—they had been taken out of the country by their mother, on a visit to England in 1965. The Itkins further avow that their trip was made on orders of the C.I.A. This claim, say government spokesmen (who insist on anonymity) is false: the C.I.A. did not send Herbert Itkin to England—a friendly land, after all—and most certainly did not send his wife there. Nevertheless, the agency obliged Itkin's attorney with a second affidavit to the effect that during the time that Itkin was acting as an informant "he and his wife went to England"—leaving open the question of whether the trip was made under C.I.A. auspices. The reason for thus fudging the matter, according to those anonymous officials, is that the C.I.A. has no wish to call Itkin a liar right out and so damage his credibility as a witness in federal court. One is left with the entertaining task of weighing the veracity of Herbert Itkin against that of the Central Intelligence Agency.

finagling to the very end, trying to use the Justice Department to resolve his domestic difficulties. (It seems probable that if the federal prosecutor could have arranged custody matters to Itkin's satisfaction, he would have. The F.B.I. showed its solicitude for the star witness in January 1968 when it arrested two men, one of whom evidently had had typically unsatisfactory business dealings with Itkin, in a plot to murder him. The federals seem to have overreached themselves. As of this writing, nearly three years after the arrest, nothing has come of the charges— "obstruction of justice"—and spokesmen at the federal courthouse have nothing intelligible to say on the subject.)

Despite everything, including a C.I.A. affidavit in the Itkins' behalf, the children remained in their father's custody; and in August 1969 Itkin gave dramatic notification to the press that he would cease his testifying if they were not taken under protective custody. Some weeks later his wife confirmed that decision. She said that her husband had received a note threatening the lives of her sons unless he stopped—and he had definitely decided to testify no more. In November the children, though still in Peekskill, had federal marshals looking after them, and Itkin was back in the witness chair, helping to send Carmine De Sapio to jail.

In the witness chair, Itkin was a prodigy, a joy to the prosecution. Given the story he had to tell, he told it in a remarkably straightforward and coherent way—while his restless eyes roamed the courtroom, assessing the effects of his recital on jury, reporters, spectators. He bore the slings of the defense attorneys stolidly, conceding the details of his disorderly past in an impersonal, almost cordial manner. Now and then, in an even voice, he corrected a mistaken date or amount of money. Nothing escaped him, little moved him.

He proved a particular torment to Carmine De Sapio's attorney, Maurice Edelbaum, celebrated for his success in keeping high-level Mafiosi at large. The star defendant De Sapio endured the weeks of trial like an already beaten man. The hunched shoulders, the grayish skin, the thin, wintry smile and the thinning, whitening hair rising still to its pathetic pompadour, the nervous hands, one holding always a crumpled handkerchief which he applied now and again to his lips and eyes—he looked more than his sixty-one years. At last the dark glasses were a sign of illness, not of mystery. He never allowed himself a glance at the infamous Corallo, his admirer,* and to all the charges against him he pleaded innocent, declaring most forcefully: "Absolutely not!" "That's ridiculous!" "That's absurd!" Asked by an assistant district attorney about his alleged part in the Con Edison conspiracy, De Sapio replied, "I wouldn't do that thirty years ago, when I was an amateur." Testimony by Max Ulrich he attributed to a possible misinterpretation. Testimony by Gerald Hadden he described as untruthful. As for Herbert Itkin's damning testimony—"It never happened." "That couldn't be possible." "Definitely lying." "Complete fabrication." "Just a complete invention." "I think Mr. Itkin is very careless with the truth."

* The proximity of Corallo at the defendants' table did nothing to improve De Sapio's morale or his chances of acquittal. As Murray Kempton remarked at Corallo's indictment, to see Tony Ducks "is to remember how impossible it was for a devil to get a fair trial in the Middle Ages." The third defendant, Henry Fried, had his trial postponed owing to illness. Gerald Hadden was granted immunity from prosecution and became a major government witness.

But Itkin could not be shaken. For four days of cross-examination, pudgy and pugnacious lawyer Edelbaum pretended that after a career spent in the service of racketeers he was offended at having to be in the same room with a person of Itkin's stripe. Mean-eyed and screeching, moving heavily from sarcasm ("Do I understand by that answer, sir, that you weren't interested in gaining any monetary advantage for yourself?") to flat disgust, for four days he went at Itkin, growling, snarling, snapping, and left no mark. The witness, never visibly annoyed, held to his story, and ferocious Edelbaum slunk away at last, frustrated and befuddled, no recourse left for his final plea to the jury but to inveigh against the sin of convicting a man like Carmine De Sapio on the word of a man like Herbert Itkin.

Itkin's accomplishment as a witness may be measured in the simplest terms. In the reservoir case, James Marcus was sentenced to fifteen months in prison; Antonio Corallo to three years; Daniel J. Motto and Henry Fried to two years each.* Corallo was sentenced to a four-and-a-half-year prison term in the Con Edison case—to run concurrently with the earlier sentence—and Carmine De Sapio was sentenced to two years. At this writing, Henry Fried has still to be tried for his part in the conspiracy. The Itkin scorecard also contains entries regarding James Plumeri

---

* In affirming the convictions of Corallo, Motto, and Fried in behalf of a unanimous Court of Appeals, Judge Harold R. Medina wrote: "And so the sorry story of the corruption of a public official comes to a close. We see politicians hovering in the background, a labor leader as the master of ceremonies and underworld characters weaving a web of intrigue in the midst of secrecy and stealth. These sinister figures chisel in on one another in the fixing of their respective shares of the loot, and finally submit to the power of one who wanted his share 'from off the top.' This record reeks with proof of the guilt of every one of those whom the jury found guilty as charged." Affirmed.

and other confederates involved in union pension-fund kickbacks, with more promised.

Marcus served most of his eleven months (taking into account time off for good behavior) at Eglin Prison Camp, a minimum security prison on Eglin Air Force Base in Fort Walton Beach, Florida, where he reached an agreement with the federal authorities to cooperate in their case against De Sapio, Corallo, and Fried, and so was spared prosecution for his own part in their plottings. He also pleaded guilty to New York City charges of conspiring to commit perjury before the grand jury, accepting a bribe in the Con Edison affair, and accepting "unlawful fees" from Vintray. This brought him a sentence of another year in prison. A loan or gift of $60,000 from an aunt of his wife in December 1967 reportedly enabled him to pay off his most pressing commitments. He and Itkin no longer see one another socially.

Gibbon wrote of "the ignominy which, in every age and country, has attended the character of an informer." The informer's special offense is not against God or against nation, and indeed has usually been performed in the ostensible service of one or the other. What disturbs us about him is that he betrays a relationship, between men, that comes closer to our common experience than the relationship between a man and his god or a man and his society. He nods and smiles and elicits confidences and then betrays, and it seems scarcely any mitigation that those whom he betrays are so often worthy of so little trust themselves. "Marcus was weak," says Itkin of his former friend. "I just opened avenues for him he wanted to take anyway." We know that the informer turns in his pals, not for our sake, but for his own, be he zealous or merely venal. He is a stoolie; he is a squealer; and he is, lawmen agree, indispensable. In a crime that involves the bribing of a public official, where the injured party is that vague entity known as The Public and the injury is not even felt until it is exposed, and not felt very deeply then, evidence must come from among the conspirators themselves. If an Itkin offends our sensibilities, we have the choice of tolerating a Plumeri.

We had best leave to the novelist or the psychoanalyst the sorting out of the motives, the hallucinations, the rationalizations of Herbert Itkin, an inveterate confidence man whose personal life was as tangled as what passed for his professional life. To borrow an epigram of Macaulay's, "He played innumerable parts, and overacted them all."

Listening to Itkin today is a heady experience.* His voice deep and controlled, his manner low-keyed and plausible, he relates a consistent narrative of his career, a madly consistent narrative: From the mid-nineteen-fifties until 1967, he was an undercover government agent—on the payroll of the C.I.A., a volunteer for the F.B.I.—unwaveringly dedicated to the national interest and the battle against crime: "If the two of us die," he says, referring to his second wife, who, he asserts, also went forth on C.I.A. missions, "we want to do it for a cause." His zeal in his

---

* Itkin granted the interview after several months of being badgered for it. He attributed the delay to the time it took him, in cooperation with the F.B.I., to run a check on my background. In response to my inquiry as to whether the F.B.I. actually carried out such a check, J. Edgar Hoover wrote: ". . . the FBI is strictly an investigative agency of the Federal Government and, as such, does not conduct background inquiries based on requests from private citizens. I can assure you this Bureau would not make an exception to this long-standing policy if it were asked to do so by Mr. Itkin."

cause has brought him unkindness from all sides. James Marcus spoiled his hopes for Conestoga. His first wife blackmailed him and raided his safe-deposit box. ("Money is very important to her.") His father-in-law inveigled him into dubious enterprises and his mother-in-law attempted to defraud him. ("I wanted no more to do with the family if I could help it.") Charles Rappaport made off with his checkbook. Another associate withheld a client's funds, and he (Itkin) was blamed. His fellow conspirators double-crossed him. The district attorney has declared a vendetta against him. ("If anybody has hurt me with the children, it's the state.") Westchester Family Court, in collusion with his wife's former husband, has deprived him of his stepchildren. The press has been unfair. ("I don't see why people can't give me the edge.") In this corrupt place and age, no one can recognize an honest man. Well, almost no one. Tony Ducks has said of Itkin, according to Itkin, "This kid is square and honest."

Names drop from his lips—Joe McCarthy, Wayne Morse ("I love him"), Harold Stassen, Allen Dulles—but instead of adding weight to his story, they float off along with his references to gold smuggling in England and airfields in the Dominican Republic. Asked for details, he speaks of security. As he goes matter-of-factly on, only his chain-smoking suggesting any inner tension or disquiet, one comes to understand that he has woven all the scattered bits and pieces of his life, all the finagling and all the woolgathering, into a pattern that is to him seamless. He has done the artist's work, adjusting the past, reshaping it, re-creating it until the world seems comprehensible and reality becomes one with the dream.

The confidence man is very much a contemporary figure, yet he belongs to a more romantic age, possessed as he is of an ever-questing spirit that can find no home port. He wants everything, the rewards of crime and the approbation of society, and he wants it all at once. He even wants the pleasures of mortification and redemption: "I figure I've got about five years before they, the Mafia or somebody else, try to kill me. Before they do, I'm going to tell the truth about what I've done and what I've seen because doing that is going to be the one really good thing I'll ever do in my lousy life."

There is some poetry in Itkin's crazy career, and it has been closed by a stupendous piece of poetic justice. For as far into the future as he can now look, the color-blind, diabetic *Luftmensch* will be grounded in protective custody, the state which he cheated and then served guarding him from the criminals whom he served and betrayed. The swinger who once traveled the world cannot set foot alone on a public street. The operator who once sold shares in the Dominican Republic and the City of New York must depend on a government dole—$86 a week plus lodging. (Yet perhaps, just perhaps, there is a hundred thousand dollars in bullion cached somewhere, and Itkin the operator will one day take to the air again.)

It is tempting to adopt the sentimental view that Itkin, like those egregious sinners of other times who came to peace in a desert, has now been compelled to find the repose that always eluded him, teaching the children on his military base to swim and play football. Capable of infinite moods, at moments he succumbs to a surface fatalism: "My life's over after this. This was my mission, and I've completed it. I'm satisfied. I just want my kids to know." But it requires a considerable effort to persuade oneself that, deep down, what Herbert Itkin has been in search of all these years has much resemblance to peace. He remains the ultimate con man, having succeeded for now in conning himself out of everything but a shadow of existence.

So our narrative ends, satisfying as a novel by Dickens. The knaves and rascals have been exposed and humiliated. The principles of honest government have been redeemed. Good citizens of New York may again rest secure in the certain knowledge that their city's affairs are in reliable hands.

Note

As most of the principals in our story could find no incentive to speak of their affairs to an outsider, and certainly not to speak of them truthfully, the preceding account is based largely on the records of their trials. As a means of writing history, that has its drawbacks. Not all the defendants testified at the trials, and those who did testify did not invariably tell the truth; the prosecutors and the defense attorneys, doing their jobs, abused hyperbole; the law suppressed certain information—and those things which jurors may not hear can be of surpassing interest to ordinary citizens. Like any juror, the student of a trial transcript may be misled on certain points. All of this being acknowledged, nonetheless the trials still open to us as detailed a look as we are likely to get into the methods of contemporary civic corruption and the personalities of a choice set of corrupters.

Our story, then, is drawn in the main from the two criminal trials in which James Marcus figured—U.S. *v.* Antonio Corallo *et al.* (67 Cr. 1051) and U.S. *v.* Carmine De Sapio *et al.* (68 Cr. 1012). A score of other indictments, trials, convictions, and appeals have also been informative. Of the many newspaper articles related to the cases, the most interesting for their information on the backgrounds of James Marcus and Herbert Itkin have been the reports in *The New York Times* by Martin Arnold and Barnard Collier. These appeared on March 9, 1968; June 24, 1968; and December 15, 1969.

A few pertinent recent books on the workings and misworkings of New York City: *At the Pleasure of the Mayor,* by Theodore J. Lowi (New York, 1964); *Behind Closed Doors,* by Edward Costikyan (New York, 1966); *Tigers of Tammany,* by Alfred Connable and Edward Silberfarb (New York, 1966); *The Tweed Ring,* by Alexander B. Callow (New York, 1966); *What Have You Done for Me Lately?,* by Warren Moscow (New York, 1967). Still more pertinent, if less recent, are the observations of James Bryce, Alexis de Tocqueville, and Lincoln Steffens. The published sources have been supplemented with interviews, where possible. The most eminent of the parties who ignored or declined requests for an interview was his honor, the Mayor of New York. Of those who helped, no one was more helpful than my editor and friend Henry Robbins.

Index

223